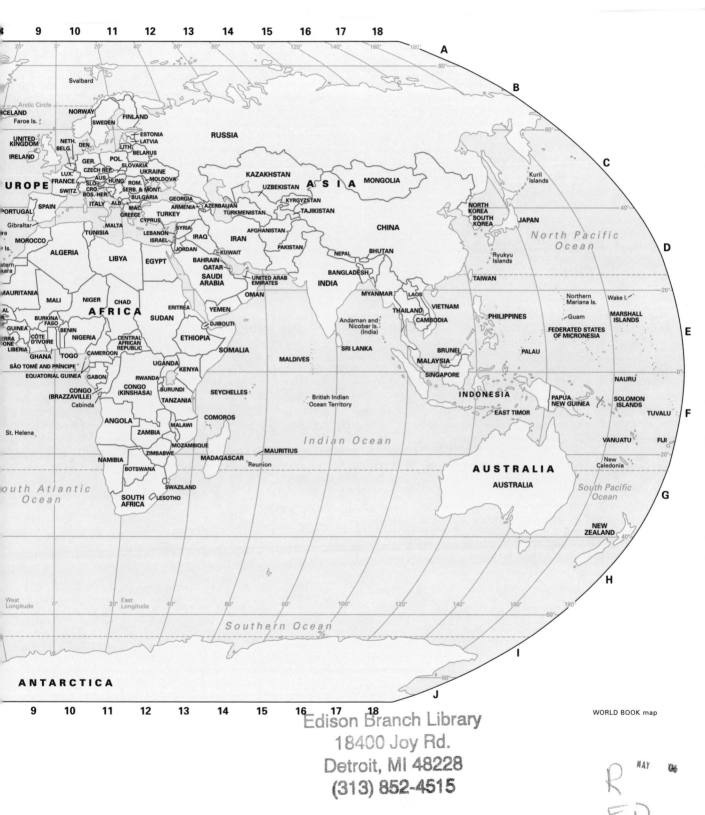

WORLD BOOK map

WORLD BOOK'S ENCYCLOPEDIA OF FLAGS

Volume 12
International Organizations
Regions
Heraldry and Symbols
Index

World Book, Inc.
a Scott Fetzer company
Chicago

Project Consultant: Whitney Smith, Ph.D., Director, Flag Research Center

For information about other World Book publications, visit our
Web site **http://www.worldbook.com** or call **1-800-WORLDBK (967-5325).**
For information about sales to schools and libraries,
call **1-800-975-3250 (United States); 1-800-837-5365 (Canada).**

World Book, Inc.
233 N. Michigan Ave.
Chicago, IL 60601 U.S.A.

Printed in the United States of America

1 2 3 4 5 6 7 8 9 10 09 08 07 06 05

Library of Congress Cataloging-in-Publication Data

World Book's encyclopedia of flags.
        p. cm.
    Includes bibliographical references and index.
    ISBN 0-7166-7900-0
    1. Flags. I.Title: Encyclopedia of flags.
CR101.W67 2005
929.9'2'03—dc22

2005004286

Additional Resources

Corcoran, Michael. *For Which It Stands.*
    Simon & Schuster, 2002.

Crampton, William G. *Flag.* 1989. Reprint.
    Dorling Kindersley, 2000.

Shearer, Benjamin F. and Barbara S.
    State Names, Seals, Flags, and Symbols. 3rd ed.
    Greenwood, 2001.

Smith, Whitney. *Flag Lore of All Nations.*
    Millbrook, 2001.

Woodcock, Thomas, and Robinson, J.M. *The
    Oxford Guide to Heraldry.* 1988. Reprint.
    Oxford, 1990.

Volume Contents

How to Use This Set 5

African Union 8
Arab League. 9
Association of Southeast Asian Nations
    (ASEAN) 10
Caribbean Community and
    Common Market (CARICOM) 11
Commonwealth of
    Independent States (CIS). 12
Commonwealth of Nations 13
European Union (EU). 14
International Red Cross and
    Red Crescent Movement 16
North Atlantic Treaty
    Organization (NATO) 18
Olympic Movement 20
Organization of American States (OAS) . . 21
Organization of Petroleum
    Exporting Countries (OPEC). 22
Pacific Community. 23
United Nations (UN) 24
World Organization of
    the Scout Movement. 26
World Association of Girl Guides
    and Girl Scouts. 27

Antarctica 28
Palestinian Authority 30
Somaliland. 31
Turkish Republic of Northern Cyprus. . . . 32
Western Sahara. 33
Liberation Colors 34
Pan-African Colors 35
Pan-Arab Colors. 36
Pan-Slavic Colors 37
International Alphabet Flags 38
International Numeral Pennants 40
U.S. Navy Numeral Flags 41
Heraldry 42
Symbols
    Cross. 44
    Fleur-de-lis 46
    Crescent and Star 48
    Sun 50
    Animals 52
    Stars 54
    Tools 56
    Plants 58

Index. 60

Set Contents

Volume 1
Afghanistan to Belgium

Volume 2
Belize to Canada — Canadian Provinces and Territories

Volume 3
Cape Verde to Equatorial Guinea

Volume 4
Eritrea to Ireland

Volume 5
Israel to Malta

Volume 6
Marshall Islands to Oman

Volume 7
Pakistan to Serbia and Montenegro

Volume 8
Seychelles to Uganda

Volume 9
Ukraine to United Kingdom — U.K. Territories and Historical Flags

Volume 10
United States — Individual States

Volume 11
United States Territories
Historical Flags of the United States
Uruguay to Zimbabwe

Volume 12
Selected International Organizations
Other Regions
Heraldry and Symbols
Index

HOW TO USE THIS SET

The 12 volumes of *World Book's Encyclopedia of Flags* contain articles on flags of every nation in the world. The flags are arranged alphabetically, from Afghanistan in Volume 1 to Zimbabwe in Volume 11. The set also includes selected historical flags and flags of organizations and political groups. Volume 12 includes an index for quick access to all entries.

In each volume, entries for individual countries and their flags are presented on two pages. The first page of each entry contains the country's history and a box listing the nation's capital, head of government, size (in area), major religions, and other important, up-to-date national data. A map in the upper right corner shows the nation's location. Also included on the first page is the history of the nation's flag.

The second page of each entry shows a large color illustration of the national flag and a data box containing key facts about the flag. These facts include a description of the banner and its width-to-length ratio. Certain countries have one flag that is used only by the government, to be flown on public buildings and used for other official purposes (a state flag), and a separate flag for use by private citizens (a civil flag). These instances are noted in the flag data box, and the flag shown will most often be the state flag.

In some volumes, readers will also find state and territory flags for certain countries. The 50 U.S. states can be found in Volume 10, for example, and the five U.S. territories follow in Volume 11. Volume 11 also contains historical American flags that illustrate the development of the United States from a colony to a modern nation.

❶ **Page numbers** are prominently displayed for easy reference.

❷ **Entry titles** appear in the colored bar at the top of the page.

❸ **Blue discs** at the beginning of entries contain map coordinates keyed to a world map on the endpapers.

❹ **Historical information** about the nation, state, or territory provides important background material.

❺ **Flag histories** explain how the banner was created.

❻ **Locator maps** show the location of a place within its region.

❼ **Data boxes** contain easy-to-access facts.

❽ **Flags** of each country are shown in large size.

❾ **Flag data boxes** include a description of the banner and its width-to-length ratio.

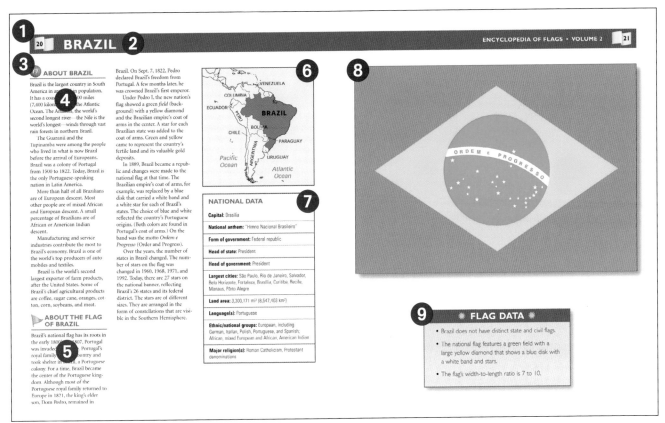

THE PARTS OF A FLAG

Special terms are sometimes used when discussing a flag. The flag's background, for example, is known as the *field*. The field is almost always a single color.

The part of the flag closest to the staff is known as the *hoist*. This is the side of the flag that is hoisted up the flagstaff. The free end of a flag, farthest from the staff, is called the *fly*. Some nations add a *badge*, or emblem, on the fly end of their banner.

The upper corner of a flag, next to the staff, is called the *canton*. Some nations and organizations include a symbol or badge in the cantons of their flags. For example, the banners of nations or other areas that were once part of the United Kingdom often include the British flag, called the Union Jack, in the canton, as does this provincial flag of Ontario that is shown, *right*.

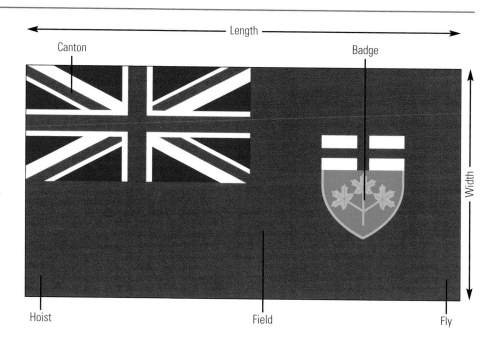

FLAG SHAPES

Flags come in different shapes and sizes. Most national banners—such as the flag of Mexico, shown in the upper left image, are *rectangular* in shape and are flown horizontally (with the longest part of the banner running from left to right). Some flags have unusual shapes, however. Switzerland's flag, shown in the bottom left image, is *square*. The flag of the U.S. state of Ohio, shown in the upper right image, is *swallow-tailed* (forked at the fly end). The example from the International Alphabet flags shown at bottom right is *pennant-shaped*.

Rectangle

Swallow-tailed

Square

Pennant

RAISING THE FLAG

To raise a flag, the banner is first attached to the halyard, the rope that runs up to the top of the flagstaff. One end of the halyard is attached to the upper corner of the flag's hoist, while the other end is attached to the lower corner of the flag's hoist. The banner is then raised to the top of the staff by pulling on the lower end of the halyard. The flag of the United States should be raised quickly and lowered slowly. It should never be allowed to touch the ground.

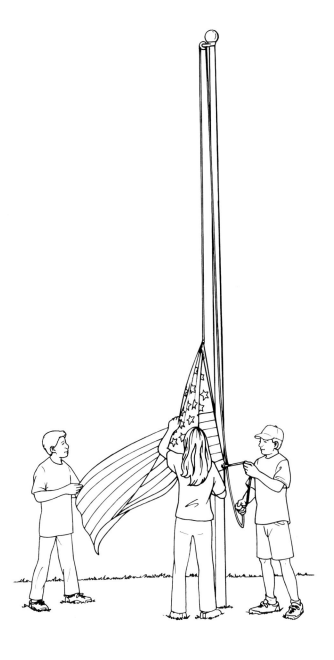

HERALDRY

Many national flags in use today were influenced by *heraldry*. Heraldry is the study of the symbols and designs used on coats of arms, flags, seals, and the like, which are used to represent families, countries, and institutions. The most important heraldic symbol is the coat of arms. Coats of arms were first used on the shields of knights. These unique symbols helped the knight's followers recognize him in battle. Today, many modern flags include a distinct coat of arms.

Over time, heraldry developed a language all its own. Shield and arms colors were called by certain names, such as purpure, an Old English word for purple. Certain symbols came to carry special meaning. A crescent, for example, represented a second son, while a rose represented a seventh son.

Although many nations have abolished heraldry because of its connection to social status and privilege, heraldic influences are still evident on flags today. For example, Mexico's flag follows the heraldic practice of separating two colors by a white or yellow line.

This shield shows a *saltire* (diagonal cross)—a design that appears in a number of modern flags.

The standard of Sir Henry Stafford, from around 1475. The Cross of St. George at the hoist identifies this as English.

KEY TO COLOR BARS

Each flag entry is bordered by a color-coded bar that allows readers to quickly identify the type of flag being covered. Blue bars represent national flags, while red bars symbolize states, provinces, or internal territories. Teal bars are used to denote certain types of territories, including overseas territories, autonomous regions, and dependencies. Some regions are also represented by a green bar. In addition, green bars are used to denote historical flags that were important in past times or flags that have influenced the development of modern flags. Purple bars represent banners used by international organizations.

NATIONAL

STATES, PROVINCES, TERRITORIES

DEPENDENCIES, REGIONS

HISTORICAL

INTERNATIONAL ORGANIZATIONS

 ## ABOUT THE FLAG OF THE AFRICAN UNION

In 1963, the Organization of African Unity (OAU) was founded in Addis Ababa, Ethiopia, with 32 members. The organization's *charter* (a written document setting forth the group's purpose and goals) was signed on May 25, a date now known as Africa Day, or African Liberation Day. In 2000, OAU leaders signed an act creating an African Union, with a structure similar to that of the European Union. The African Union officially replaced the OAU on July 9, 2002.

On July 8, 2004, the African Union chose to continue using the previous OAU banner. That flag has five horizontal stripes—green, gold, white, gold, and green. A logo is shown on the middle white stripe. The colors were chosen to symbolize ideals. Green represents the hope for unity. Gold symbolizes the wealth and bright future of Africa. White stands for the purity of Africa's desire to live in friendship with all countries. The logo features a gold map of the continent of Africa, without country borders, surrounded by green and gold circles and flanked by palm leaves representing peace. Small red rings linked at the base of the logo stand for African solidarity and refer to the blood shed by Africans in the fight for freedom over the past years. The width-to-length ratio of the flag is 2 to 3.

ABOUT THE FLAG OF THE ARAB LEAGUE

The Arab League began using its current flag in 1945, the same year in which the league was created. The flag is green, with the league's emblem in the center.

In Islam, green is associated with Fatima, the daughter of the Prophet Muhammad who founded the religion. Green is used in the national flags of many Arab countries, including five of the seven original Arab League members. Green also represents the fertile areas around the region's most important rivers—the Nile, Tigris, and Euphrates.

The Arab League's official emblem includes the name of the organization written in white Arabic letters. The white crescent below the letters is a traditional Muslim symbol. The golden yellow chain that encircles the letters and crescent stands for cooperation among Arab countries. The white wreath encircling the yellow chain is said to represent peace and to suggest the prosperity of Arab lands. The flag has a width-to-length ratio of 1 to 2 or 2 to 3.

ABOUT THE FLAG OF THE ASSOCIATION OF SOUTHEAST ASIAN NATIONS (ASEAN)

The Association of Southeast Asian Nations (ASEAN) was established in 1967 by five nations—Indonesia, Malaysia, the Philippines, Singapore, and Thailand. The organization's first logo had a yellow *field* (background) encircled by a blue border, with five brown rice stalks in the center and the letters *ASEAN* below in blue. After membership in ASEAN grew over the years to include 10 Southeast Asian countries, the emblem was redesigned.

The current flag, adopted on May 31, 1997, has a dark blue field and shows 10 yellow rice stalks on a red disk that is bordered in white. The colors included in the flag are the main colors of the flags of the member countries. Blue represents stability and peace. Yellow represents prosperity. Red stands for courage and energy. White symbolizes purity. The circle is said to represent unity. The flag's width-to-length ratio is 2 to 3.

ABOUT THE FLAG OF THE CARIBBEAN COMMUNITY AND COMMON MARKET (CARICOM)

The Caribbean Community and Common Market (CARICOM) was established in 1973 to encourage political and economic cooperation among Caribbean nations. The CARICOM flag was approved in 1983.

The flag's stripes—light blue over dark blue—symbolize the sky and the Caribbean Sea. The central yellow disk represents the sun. The green border around the disk stands for the vegetation of the region. The two black letter *C*'s that appear linked on the disk stand for *Caribbean Community*. The colors of the flag are found in various combinations in the national flags of the 14 CARICOM member nations. A blue *field* (background) with a central emblem is frequently used for the flags of international associations. The flag's width-to-length ratio is 2 to 3.

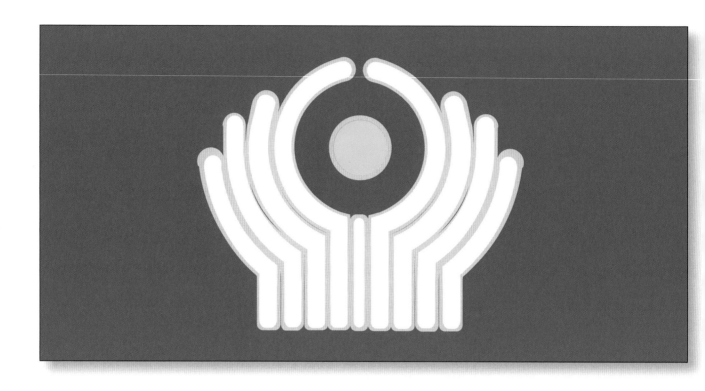

ABOUT THE FLAG OF THE COMMONWEALTH OF INDEPENDENT STATES (CIS)

In 1990, several of the 15 republics of the Union of Soviet Socialist Republics (U.S.S.R., or Soviet Union) declared independence. In August 1991, the Soviet Union began to break apart after an attempted coup. All the republics except Russia declared independence during the coup or soon after. Russia proclaimed itself the Soviet Union's successor. Some of the former Soviet republics still wanted to maintain some ties to Russia. As a result, the Commonwealth of Independent States (CIS) was established in December 1991. The new commonwealth initially included 11 former republics of the Soviet Union—Armenia, Azerbaijan, Belarus, Kazakhstan, Kyrgyzstan, Moldova, Russia, Tajikistan, Turkmenistan, Ukraine, and Uzbekistan. Georgia joined the CIS in 1993.

A flag for the CIS was introduced on April 15, 1994, and officially adopted on Jan. 19, 1996. Russian artist Alexander Wasilijewitsch Grigorjew, the flag's designer, chose a blue *field* (background) to symbolize peace and spirituality. The yellow disk in the center represents light, warmth, life, and eternal values. The white central emblem, which resembles the columns of a cathedral, stands for a common gathering place where people cooperate. The emblem can also be viewed as a tree, strong and growing. The design of the flag as a whole suggests stability and unity. The flag's width-to-length ratio is 1 to 2.

ABOUT THE FLAG OF THE COMMONWEALTH OF NATIONS

The British Commonwealth of Nations was formed in the early 1900's and legalized by British law in 1931. As original members, the former British colonies of Canada, Australia, Ireland, New Zealand, Newfoundland, and South Africa were recognized as independent countries that were equal in rank to and freely associated with the United Kingdom. Between 1947 and 1980, about 40 more British colonies became independent nations. Nearly all of them joined the Commonwealth. During this time, Ireland gave up its membership, and Newfoundland became a province of Canada.

A flag was adopted for the Commonwealth of Nations on March 26, 1976. The banner features a blue *field* (background) with a yellow globe in the center. The globe, made up of lines of longitude and latitude, is surrounded by yellow rays, or spears, that form the letter *C*. The rays symbolize the many facets of Commonwealth cooperation around the world. There is no symbolism associated with the colors.

EUROPEAN UNION (EU)

 ABOUT THE FLAG OF THE EUROPEAN UNION (EU)

After World War II (1939–1945), Europeans were eager to promote peace and unity throughout the region. To that aim, a group called the Council of Europe was formed in 1949. On Sept. 25, 1953, the organization adopted a blue flag with a ring of 15 yellow stars in the center. The blue symbolized the sky, while the 15 stars represented the 15 member nations. Germany, however, opposed the flag because one of the stars represented a territory called Saarland that France had taken from Germany after the war. On Dec. 9, 1955, the council approved a flag with 12 stars. The stars represent all European peoples, while their number symbolizes perfection and unity rather than the number of members.

On May 26, 1986, the European Community (EC) adopted the banner of the Council of Europe as its own. In 1992, EC members signed the Maastricht Treaty, which provided for the creation of the European Union (EU). The treaty took effect in November 1993. The banner of the EC then became the official flag of the European Union. Today, both the EU and the Council of Europe use the flag.

☀ FLAG DATA ☀

- The flag of the European Union features a dark blue *field* (background) with a circle of 12 yellow stars in the center.

- The flag's width-to-length ratio is 1 to 1½.

ABOUT THE FLAGS OF THE INTERNATIONAL RED CROSS AND RED CRESCENT MOVEMENT

The flag of the Red Cross became internationally recognized in 1864, when the first Geneva Convention, or Treaty, went into effect. The Geneva Conventions are a series of agreements that provide rules for the treatment of wounded and sick military personnel in the field; for the care of wounded, sick, and shipwrecked members of the armed forces at sea; and for the humane treatment of prisoners of war. The conventions also provide for the protection of civilians and members of militias and volunteer corps during wartime. The first Geneva Convention thus protected the Red Cross and, later, the Red Crescent groups that provided wartime medical services.

Jean Henri Dunant (1828–1910), a Swiss philanthropist, founded the International Red Cross. The name Red Cross comes from the organization's flag, a red cross on a white *field* (background). This design was chosen on Oct. 26, 1863, at a conference of delegates from 16 nations and several charitable organizations who met to discuss Dunant's idea for an international relief organization. The conference took place in Geneva, Switzerland, and the group chose to honor Switzerland by reversing the colors on the Swiss national flag (a white cross on a red background) to create its own flag. The exact design and size of the red cross and the size of the white flag on which it is shown have purposely been left undefined. Today, more than 175 nations have a Red Cross or Red Crescent society. The red crescent is used in place of the red cross on the flags of societies in most Muslim countries.

The red cross symbol is currently used by the International Committee of the Red Cross, by the International Federation of Red Cross and Red Crescent Societies, and by national Red Cross societies. Under international law, a red cross on a white flag is also a protective symbol for medical and religious workers as well as their buildings and vehicles.

In Israel, the Magen David Adom parallels, but is not affiliated with, the International Red Cross. The Israeli society uses a white flag bearing a red, six-pointed star called the Shield of David.

The Red Crescent is a relief organization that provides medical services to Muslim nations. Its purpose is similar to that of the Red Cross. The Red Cross symbol had been officially recognized in 1864. However, a cross was unacceptable to Muslims in the Turkish-ruled Ottoman Empire because of that symbol's similarity to the emblem used by Christian Crusaders of Western Europe who had fought Turks and other Muslims from the late 1000's to the 1500's. The crescent, a symbol of Islam, was then chosen to replace the cross on flags used in Muslim lands. The red crescent symbol was first used in 1876.

The flag of the Red Crescent—a white *field* (background) with a red crescent in the center—is widely used in Muslim countries today. However, some of the flags show the crescent facing left, while others show it facing right. The exact shape, size, and direction of the crescent are intentionally not specified under international law.

Because of the large Muslim population in the Soviet Union, a nation that existed from 1922 to 1991, that country used a banner with a combination of a red cross and a red crescent. For many years, proposals for a new, single symbol for the entire Red Cross and Red Crescent Movement have been discussed. However, no such symbol has been decided upon.

ABOUT THE FLAG OF THE NORTH ATLANTIC TREATY ORGANIZATION (NATO)

The North Atlantic Treaty Organization (NATO) was established in 1949 as a military alliance consisting of the United States, Canada, and a group of Western European nations. Originally, the central purpose of NATO was to discourage an attack by the Communist-led Soviet Union on the non-Communist nations of Western Europe. Since the breakup of the Soviet Union in 1991, the main focus of NATO has shifted toward international crisis management and peacekeeping. A number of former Soviet republics and countries in Eastern Europe joined NATO in 2004.

The NATO flag was approved on Oct. 14, 1953. It has been flown at NATO headquarters, on ships, and in ceremonies. The dark blue *field* (background) represents the Atlantic Ocean. The white-and-blue emblem in the center is called a *compass rose*. The four-pointed star of the compass rose symbolizes the member nations' common goal of peace. The emblem's ring is a symbol of unity.

☀ FLAG DATA ☀

- The NATO flag features a dark blue field with a white-and-blue compass rose centered within a white circle.

- The flag's width-to-length ratio is 3 to 4.

 ## ABOUT THE FLAG OF THE OLYMPIC MOVEMENT

The Olympic flag was displayed for the first time in 1914, on the 20th anniversary of the founding of the International Olympic Committee (IOC). The first time it was raised at an Olympic Games occurred at the 1920 Olympics in Antwerp, Belgium. The banner was designed by a French educator, Baron Pierre de Coubertin, who developed the modern Olympic movement. The flag has a white *field* (background) with five equal, interlocking rings of blue, yellow, black, green, and red. The blue, black, and red rings rest above the yellow and green rings. The five ring colors and the white of the field were said to have been chosen because they included the national flag colors of all of the countries that participated in the first five modern Olympic Games. The rings later came to be associated with Africa, Asia, Australia, Europe, and the Americas.

The Olympic flag plays a prominent role at each Summer and Winter games. After the lighting of the Olympic flame during the Opening Ceremony, the flag bearers of the participating nations gather around a person from the host nation who serves as a representative of all the athletes in the games. This person holds the Olympic flag with the left hand and raises the right hand while taking the Olympic oath. The Olympic flag flies throughout the Olympics and is lowered at the end of the games. At the closing ceremony, the mayor of the host city hands the official Olympic flag to the IOC president, who then passes it to the mayor of the city that will host the next Olympics.

In addition to flying the traditional Olympic flag, the Olympic organizing committee of the city hosting the games often flies its own special banner. These special banners usually incorporate a version of the five-ring Olympic logo.

The image of the Olympic flag and its ring logo are protected by law in nearly every nation. This legal protection prevents the banner and logo from being misused by unauthorized individuals or groups. Since the late 1980's, the IOC has earned money by licensing reproductions of the flag or logo for such products as commemorative coins and stamps. The flag's width-to-length ratio is 2 to 3.

ABOUT THE FLAG OF THE ORGANIZATION OF AMERICAN STATES (OAS)

The Organization of American States (OAS) is an association of 35 American countries that seeks to provide for collective self-defense, regional cooperation, and the peaceful settlement of controversies in the Americas. The OAS had its early beginning at the First International Conference of American States, which met in Washington, D.C., in 1889 and 1890. The delegates established the International Union of American Republics, with the Commercial Bureau of the American Republics as its central office. In 1910, this bureau was renamed the Pan American Union. In 1948, the Pan American Union became the permanent body of the OAS. In 1970, the Pan American Union was renamed the General Secretariat of the OAS.

The emblem in the center of the OAS flag may have been used as early as the 1920's. The OAS flag is a blue banner that bears a white disk bordered in gold or yellow. The disk shows a small section of each member state's national flag, arranged in a circle. Ten flagpoles stand at the bottom. As new countries have joined the OAS, the flag's design has been altered to add their flag to the emblem. The flags are arranged clockwise in Spanish alphabetical order. The OAS has not adopted any official regulations concerning the dimensions of its flag.

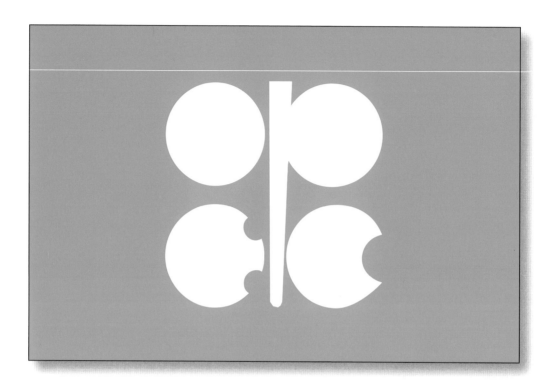

ABOUT THE FLAG OF THE ORGANIZATION OF PETROLEUM EXPORTING COUNTRIES (OPEC)

The Organization of Petroleum Exporting Countries (OPEC) was officially established on Sept. 14, 1960. The organization is an association of 11 nations that depend heavily on oil exports for their income. The OPEC flag, designed in 1970, is light blue with a white *logo* (emblem) in the center. The logo is made up of four white disks. Each disk has been designed so that together they form the organization's initials. The flag's light blue *field* (background) was chosen to match the blue of the United Nations flag.

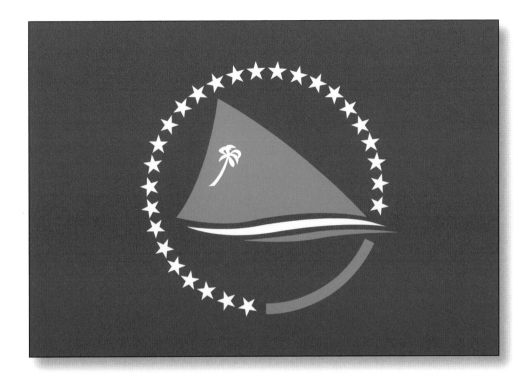

ABOUT THE FLAG OF THE PACIFIC COMMUNITY

In 1947, six colonial powers created the South Pacific Commission (SPC) to promote the economic and social welfare of the Pacific Islands. Today, it includes independent island nations as well as countries that administer Pacific islands.

Early versions of the SPC flag had a light blue background and an arc of six-pointed gold stars to symbolize the Pacific Ocean and the SPC members. A white palm tree was also included. The basic design was modified a number of times over the years, and additional stars were placed in the ring of the flag emblem as new members joined the SPC.

In 1997, the organization changed its name from the South Pacific Commission to the Pacific Community. The current flag of the Pacific Community has a dark blue *field* (background) with 27 white, five-pointed stars. The deep blue color is said to stand for the clear night skies of the Pacific region. The turquoise-blue sail is said to represent the island chains of the region as well as the ideas of youth, movement, and change. The palm tree is said to symbolize wealth. The ring of stars is said to resemble an *atoll* (ring-shaped coral island).

ABOUT THE FLAG OF THE UNITED NATIONS (UN)

In April 1945, near the end of World War II (1939–1945), representatives from 50 nations gathered at a conference in San Francisco. The representatives were given "smoke-blue" buttons to wear on their clothing. The design on the buttons showed a simplified map of the world with the North Pole in the center. Olive branches surrounding the world emblem represented peace. The design symbolized the worldwide scope of the new United Nations (UN). The design was created by members of the Presentation Branch of the United States Office of Strategic Services.

On Oct. 15, 1946, the General Assembly of the United Nations decided to adopt an emblem and a seal that could be used to represent the United Nations. Modifications were made to the design used for the conference buttons.

The new design was adopted as the emblem of the United Nations on Dec. 7, 1946. It consisted of a smoke-blue *field* (background) with the map's land areas and the olive branches in gold and the water areas in white. Unofficially, a flag was used showing this design in white on a blue field, with the words *United Nations* in English and French surrounding it. That banner was first displayed in 1947 by a UN group working in Greece. A flag of the same design without the inscription was adopted by the UN General Assembly on Oct. 20, 1947.

✸ FLAG DATA ✸

- The flag of the United Nations features a smoke-blue background with a world map centered on the North Pole, surrounded by olive branches, in white.

- The flag's width-to-length ratio is 2 to 3 or 3 to 5.

 ## ABOUT THE FLAG OF THE WORLD ORGANIZATION OF THE SCOUT MOVEMENT

Robert Baden-Powell, a British Army officer, started the Boy Scout movement in 1907. Its popularity eventually led to the founding of the World Organization of the Scout Movement, an international organization based in Geneva, Switzerland. Today, there are more than 28 million Scouts worldwide, including both male and female members.

The World Scout Flag has a purple *field* (background) and bears the organization's emblem. A white rope, which represents the strength and unity of scouting around the world, is tied in a *reef* (square) knot encircling a white *trefoil* (three-leaved) emblem. A purple star appears on each of the trefoil's two outer leaves. The stars stand for knowledge and truth. According to Baden-Powell, the trefoil emblem is a *fleur-de-lis* (a design representing an iris), similar to one shown on a compass. It was chosen as a Scouting symbol because it suggests that Scouting, like the compass, always shows the right direction for moving forward. Baden-Powell believed that the trefoil was a symbol of peace and purity, with three points for the three parts of the Scout Oath. The Scout Oath includes a duty to God and country, a duty to other people, and a duty to one's self.

ABOUT THE FLAG OF THE WORLD ASSOCIATION OF GIRL GUIDES AND GIRL SCOUTS

The World Association of Girl Guides and Girl Scouts was organized in London in 1928. Today, it has a membership of about 10 million girls and young women.

In 1930, the Girl Scout World Conference adopted what was known as the World Flag. The banner, designed by Kari Aas of Norway, had a blue *field* (background) and featured a yellow *trefoil* (three-leaved) clover emblem bearing a blue compass needle and two blue stars. The trefoil was similar to the one designed earlier for the Boy Scouts by that movement's founder, the British Army officer Robert Baden-Powell. The compass needle at the center of the Girl Guides/Girl Scouts trefoil is meant to suggest that Scouting, like the compass, always points the right direction for moving forward. The stars of the World Flag stand for the Promise and Laws of the movement.

In May 1991, the flag was redesigned. The field was changed to a brighter shade of blue. A ring was added around the trefoil emblem to suggest Scouting around the world. The emblem is shown in golden yellow in the upper corner of the *hoist*—that is, the part of the flag closest to the staff. A white "blaze" framed by three golden squares appears in the lower corner of the *fly*—that is, the free end of the flag, farthest from the staff. The white color symbolizes a commitment to world peace, while the squares stand for the three parts of the Girl Guide/Girl Scout promise. These three parts are to serve God and country, to help others, and to live by the Girl Scout Law. The Girl Scout Law outlines many positive qualities and behaviors, including honesty, consideration, courage, respect, and wise use of resources.

ABOUT THE FLAG OF ANTARCTICA

On Dec. 14, 1911, explorers from Norway became the first people to reach the South Pole. To mark their achievement, they raised their national flag. Norway's flag was followed by the banners of many other nations whose scientists explored the continent.

Over the years, 7 countries claimed sections of Antarctica. In 1959, officials of 12 countries that had built Antarctic bases signed the Antarctic Treaty, which took effect in 1961. The terms of the treaty guaranteed that Antarctica would be used only for scientific research and other peaceful purposes. Under the treaty, the claims of the 7 countries to Antarctica were neither recognized nor rejected. Other nations later joined the treaty. In 1991, the Antarctic Treaty nations signed the Madrid Protocol, which took effect in 1998. This agreement provides further protection of the Antarctic environment and prohibits mineral exploitation. Today, more than 40 year-round scientific stations operate on the continent and nearby islands.

Antarctica has no official flag. Several unofficial flags have been designed to represent Antarctica. The earliest proposal was made in 1978. This banner, created by flag historian Whitney Smith, has an orange *field* (background) with a white emblem. Orange is often used for clothing and other purposes in Antarctica because it is easily seen against the snow and ice. The emblem appears at the *hoist*—that is, the part of the flag closest to the staff. It features a white *A* (for Antarctica), which appears above a white semicircular disk that is framed by an open pair of hands. The semicircular disk stands for the part of Earth below the South Polar Circle. The hands represent protection of the fragile environment. The area between the disk and the hands forms a dove, a symbol of peace.

Another flag proposal, created by Graham Bartram in 1996, has a light blue field with a large white emblem in the shape of the continent. The shade of blue used for the field was chosen to match the flag of the United Nations.

☀ FLAG DATA ☀

- One unofficial flag of Antarctica features a blue field with a white emblem shaped like the continent of Antarctica.

- The flag has no official width-to-length ratio.

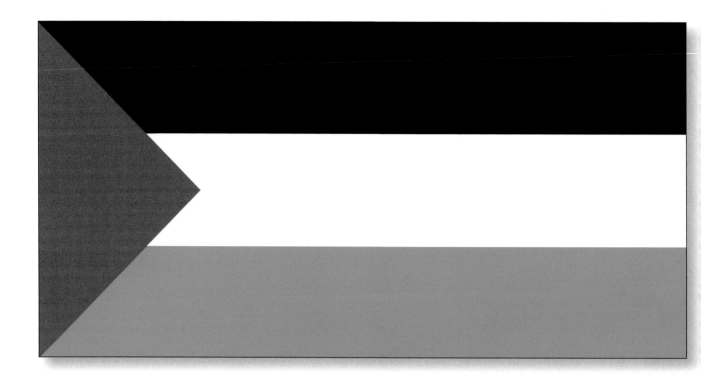

ABOUT THE FLAG OF THE PALESTINIAN AUTHORITY

In 1920, the League of Nations gave the United Kingdom a mandate to administer "Palestine." This mandated territory included the areas that today form Israel, the West Bank, and the Gaza Strip. In 1927, the British established as a civil ensign a British Red Ensign. (An *ensign* is a national flag flown by a naval ship.) The Red Ensign was defaced with a white disk inscribed with *Palestine*. This Red Ensign, the Union Jack, and a defaced British Blue Ensign were the flags used in Palestine until 1948.

The 1917 Arab Revolt Flag had been intended for a united Syria, Iraq, Lebanon, Palestine/Israel, and Jordan. It featured stripes of black, green, and white with a red triangle. These colors represented the historic Arab *dynasties* (ruling families). In 1948, after the flag's stripes were changed to black, white, and green, the Arab population of Palestine unofficially adopted this as their flag.

Since the Arab-Israeli wars of 1948 and 1967, Israel has occupied Arab Palestine. While their homeland has no internationally recognized flag or borders, Palestinians see the flag as representing their struggle for independence and statehood. It was endorsed in 1964 by the Palestinian Liberation Organization (PLO). In 1993, negotiations between Israel and the PLO over a resolution of their differences allowed for a lifting of Israeli restrictions on the flying of the Palestinian flag for the first time since 1948. The Palestinian flag features three horizontal stripes of equal width—black, white, and green—with a red triangle. It has a width-to-length ratio of 1 to 2.

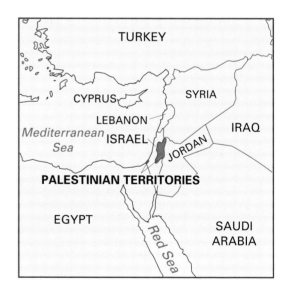

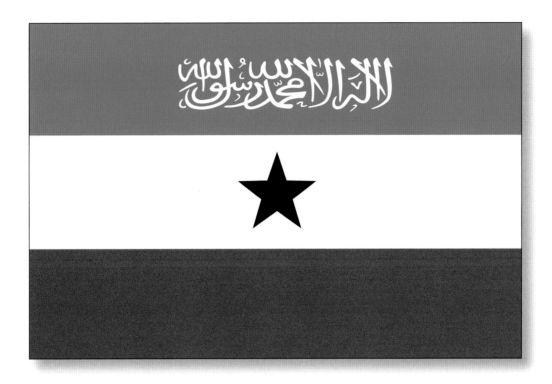

ABOUT THE FLAG OF SOMALILAND

In the late 1800's, the United Kingdom established a colony called British Somaliland. The official flag of British Somaliland was the Union Jack, the national flag of the United Kingdom. Later, the colony used the British Blue Ensign. (An *ensign* is a national flag flown by a naval ship; a British ensign is a flag with the Union Jack in the *canton*, the upper corner of a flag closest to the staff.) The flag of Somaliland featured a special emblem representing the colony in the *fly* (the free end of the flag, farthest from the staff). In 1960, British Somaliland and Italian Somaliland gained independence and united to form the Somali Republic, also known as Somalia. The northern region of Somalia became known as Somaliland.

In May 1991, during a civil war, Somaliland declared itself an independent country. Shortly thereafter, a new national banner was raised. The flag had a white *field* (background) with a lime-green disk in the center. Around the disk, inscribed in black Arabic letters, was the *shahada*—the Muslim witness of faith, which translates to: "I bear witness that there is no God but Allah. I bear witness that Muhammad is his Prophet."

On Oct. 14, 1996, the current flag was introduced. It has horizontal stripes of equal width—green, white, and red. The shahada appears in white Arabic letters in the green stripe. A black star is centered in the white stripe. The banner was based on the flag of the Somali National Movement, a political group in the region. No nation recognizes Somaliland as an independent state. Internationally, Somaliland is recognized as part of Somalia.

 **ABOUT THE FLAG OF THE TURKISH REPUBLIC OF NORTHERN CYPRUS**

In 1960, the newly independent Republic of Cyprus tried to resolve long-standing problems between the Greek majority and Turkish minority populations that lived on the island. These efforts failed, however, and in 1974 the Turkish army seized the northern section of the island. In 1975, Turkish Cypriot leaders declared this section to be an autonomous (self-governing) region called the Turkish Federated State of Cyprus. The new state flew the national flag of Turkey. On Nov. 15, 1983, the state's government proclaimed the region an independent nation, the Turkish Republic of Northern Cyprus (TRNC). The TRNC is, however, recognized only by Turkey. Other nations still consider the region to be part of Cyprus. United Nations troops patrol a buffer zone that separates the area controlled by Turkish forces and the area in which Greek Cypriots live.

In March 1984, the TRNC adopted a new national flag. The banner is based on the Turkish flag. The red star and crescent appear off-center between two red horizontal stripes on a white *field* (background). However, the flag of Turkey is still in use on Cyprus, and the government of Cyprus allows citizens to fly the Turkish flag without restriction. The width-to-length ratio of the flag of the Turkish Republic of Northern Cyprus is 2 to 3.

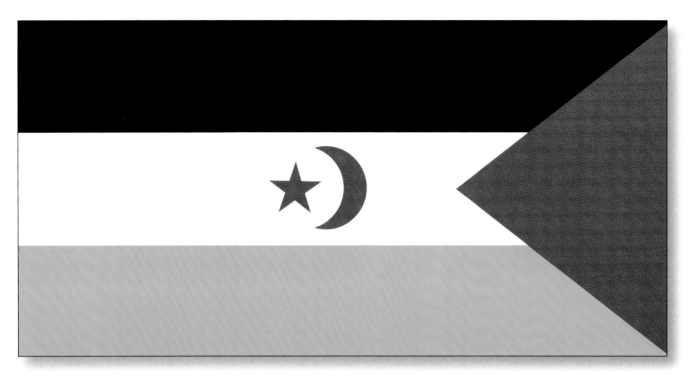

ABOUT THE FLAG OF WESTERN SAHARA

In 1976, Spain gave up the area called Spanish Sahara to Morocco and Mauritania, the two nations that flank the Spanish Sahara. Morocco claimed the northern part of Spanish Sahara, and Mauritania the southern part of the region. The area came to be called Western Sahara. In 1979, Mauritania gave up its claim, and then Morocco claimed the entire area.

On Feb. 27, 1976, an organization of people of Western Sahara, called the Polisario Front, declared the independent Saharawi Arab Democratic Republic (SADR) and formed a government-in-exile. The flag designed for the SADR is similar to that of the Palestinian Authority—the government for Palestinians in much of the Gaza Strip and West Bank. The flag has three equal horizontal stripes— black, white, and green. The SADR flag also has a red triangle at the *fly* (the free end of the flag, farthest from the staff) and bears a red star and crescent in the center. The red color stands for blood, white stands for liberty, and green symbolizes progress. Black represents the time when the region was a Spanish colony. The star and crescent represent the Islamic faith. The Polisario Front has stated that when the region wins its freedom from Morocco, the black and green stripes will be reversed in position.

A United Nations-supervised cease-fire between Polisario Front forces and Moroccan forces was declared in late 1991. The cease-fire plan also called for a *referendum* (direct vote) to determine whether Western Sahara would become independent or part of Morocco. However, disagreements between Morocco and the Polisario Front over voter eligibility have repeatedly delayed the referendum.

ABOUT THE LIBERATION COLORS

The Revolutionary War in America (1775–1783) and the French Revolution (1789–1799) offered strong models for freedom and democracy to the rest of the world. Both revolutions followed a war that liberated the Netherlands from Spanish rule in 1648. The principles of liberty, equality, and fraternity were symbolized by the red, white, and blue flags of all three countries—the Netherlands, the United States, and France.

In the 1800's and early 1900's, these red, white, and blue "colors of liberty" were chosen by many countries around the world for their own flags. The flag of Norway, using liberation colors, is shown above. The flag's width-to-length ratio is 8 to 11.

ABOUT THE PAN-AFRICAN COLORS

In 1914, the Jamaican social reformer Marcus Garvey (1887–1940) founded the Universal Negro Improvement Association. One of the group's purposes was to encourage a sense of pride among blacks everywhere. Garvey pointed to Ethiopia as an example of such pride. Ethiopia is one of the oldest independent African states. The nation's banner includes the colors red, yellow, and green.

To represent his movement, which he brought to the United States, Garvey chose a banner of black, red, and green. The black symbolized the African race, red stood for its blood, and green represented nature. Many African Americans now use this flag, which was unveiled on Aug. 13, 1920.

When Ghana became independent in 1957, it chose a flag of red, yellow, green, and black. These colors came to be known as the *pan-African* colors. As other African nations became independent, many used all or some of the pan-African colors in their flags.

The flag of Ghana, shown above, uses the pan-African colors and has a width-to-length ratio of 2 to 3.

ABOUT THE PAN-ARAB COLORS

The origins of the pan-Arab colors can be traced to the Prophet Muhammad, who founded the religion of Islam in the A.D. 600's. According to tradition, the various Muslim religious leaders who followed after the time of Muhammad each used a different-colored flag. A flag of white came to represent the Umayyad *dynasty* (family of rulers). The Abbasids used black flags when they overthrew the Umayyads in 750. Green appeared in flags used by the Fatimid dynasty, which claimed to descend from Muhammad's daughter Fatima. The color red was used by various Islamic rulers in the area. The Arab poet Safi al-Din al-Hilli wrote about the symbolism of these four colors: white for deeds, black for battlefields, green for pastures, and red for the blood of the enemy on the Arab warriors' knives or swords.

The Arab Revolt flag (shown above) was designed in 1916. The banner used the pan-Arab colors of white, black, green, and red. It had three equal horizontal stripes: black on top, green in the middle, and white on the bottom. A red triangle appeared at the *hoist*—that is, the part of the flag closest to the staff. Today, these four colors are used on the flags of many Arab countries—for instance, Iraq, Jordan, and Kuwait use these colors in their flag. Some Arab nations also use a design similar to the Arab Revolt flag. The dimensions of the Arab Revolt flag varied.

ABOUT THE PAN-SLAVIC COLORS

For many decades, Russia was the only independent *Slavic* country—that is, a nation where most of the people are *Slavs* (a group of peoples who live mainly in eastern Europe and whose languages are related). As other Slavic countries fought for their independence from foreign powers in the 1800's, they looked to Russia for help and inspiration. The Russian national tricolor of white, blue, and red horizontal stripes became the model for other Slavic ethnic and national flags.

Russia's banner had been created in 1699 by Czar Peter the Great. He used the flag of the Netherlands as his model for the Russian flag. The Dutch banner has three horizontal stripes of red, white, and blue. These three colors eventually became known as the *pan-Slavic* colors.

The pan-Slavic Congress, held in Prague, Czechoslovakia (now the Czech Republic), in 1948, may have made the use of the three pan-Slavic colors more popular. Slavs in some Austrian provinces used banners of white, blue, and red. Since the breakup of Yugoslavia in 1991–1992, the number of flags using the pan-Slavic colors has increased.

The Russian flag (shown above) uses pan-Slavic colors and has a width-to-length ratio of 2 to 3.

ABOUT THE INTERNATIONAL ALPHABET FLAGS

International alphabet flags are a set of 26 flags used by nonmilitary ships around the world to symbolize the letters of the Roman alphabet (the alphabet used in English and many other languages). Each flag represents a different letter. The flag for the letter *B*, for example, is a plain red *swallow-tailed* flag. A swallow-tailed flag is a banner that is forked at the *fly* (the free end of a flag, farthest from the staff). The flag for the letter *R* is a square red banner with a central yellow cross.

When a ship is in distress, it is customary for the crew to hoist the *N* and *C* flags together. The *N* flag is a checkered flag of blue and white. The *C* flag has five horizontal stripes—from top to bottom, blue, white, red, white, and blue.

Each alphabet flag also carries its own meaning that should be known by all mariners. The *O* flag, for example, means "man overboard." In the days before radio and other forms of instant communication, such flags could mean the difference between life and death at sea. Today, the flags are still used whenever it is necessary for ships to maintain radio silence.

*International
Alphabet Flags*

A B C D E
F G H I J K L
M N O P Q R S
T U V W X Y Z

International Numeral Pennants

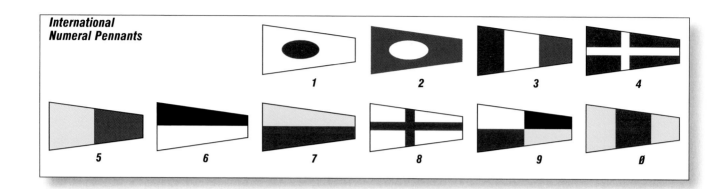

1   2   3   4

5   6   7   8   9   Ø

ABOUT THE INTERNATIONAL NUMERAL PENNANTS

International numeral pennants are a set of 10 flags used by nonmilitary ships around the world to visually represent zero and the numerals 1 through 9. The symbol on each banner represents a different number. The flag for the number one, for example, is a white banner with a red disk. All of the flags are pennant-shaped—that is, they taper toward the fly end of the flag. The flags are called "pennant one," "pennant two," and so on.

U.S. Navy Numeral Flags

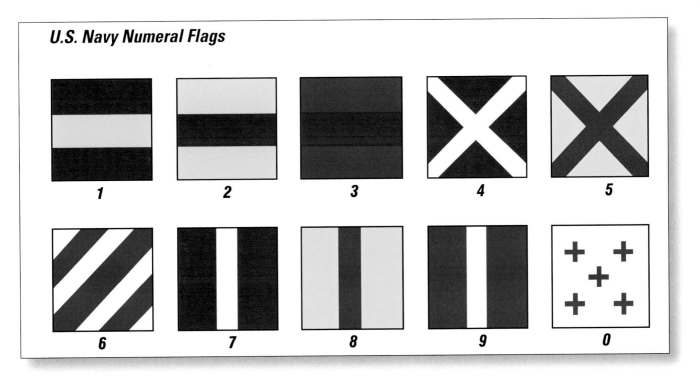

ABOUT THE U.S. NAVY NUMERAL FLAGS

In addition to using the international alphabet flags and the international numeral pennants, the United States Navy also uses its own special set of numeral flags. These 10 square flags are used to visually represent zero and the numerals 1 through 9. The banner for the number 3, for example, is blue with a horizontal red stripe across the middle.

U.S. Navy numeral flags are used when a flag message includes a number in it. When written, Navy numeral flags appear as "1" for the flag representing the number one, "2" for the flag representing the number two, and so on.

ABOUT HERALDRY

Heraldry—that is, the study of symbols used to represent individuals, families, countries, and institutions—had its start during the early 1100's. At that time, European knights wore armor made of heavy metal with helmets that covered their face. They placed *emblems* (designs) on their shields and outer coats so that their warriors could identify them during battle. Such an outer coat, also called a *surcoat*, was the original "coat of arms." The emblems were also used on flags that were carried into battle.

In peacetime, coats of arms continued to be used on banners and seals to represent upper-class individuals and families, including royalty, noblility, and clergy. The common people did not have coats of arms. In time, official messengers, called *heralds,* were given the responsibility of regulating the various emblems. Heraldic symbols provided a means of identity. Various rules and guidelines of heraldry were developed.

The earliest European flags usually followed the rules of heraldry. The banner included a shield, a *crest* (the decoration at the top of the coat of arms), and a motto. Many of these early flags contained emblems associated with symbols of the saints. In the 1200's, for example, England began using a flag that incorporated the Cross of St. George (a red cross on a white *field*, or background). Later, the flag of the United Kingdom included emblems representing the patron saints of England, Scotland, and Ireland. British territories often used the flag in combination with their own unique coat of arms.

Parts of a coat of arms

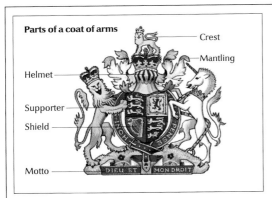

- Crest
- Mantling
- Helmet
- Supporter
- Shield
- Motto

The displaying of arms

Coats of arms were first displayed on the shields of knights. Later, arms appeared on flags, clothes, and other possessions.

WORLD BOOK illustrations by Oxford Illustrators Limited

Symbols used on a coat of arms

Coats of arms were developed during the 1100's as a way to help a knight's followers recognize him on the battlefield. The colors, designs, lines, and *cadency* (status) symbols shown below became standard and were used in different combinations according to specific rules.

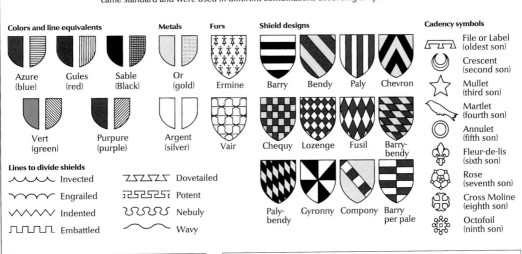

Colors and line equivalents

- Azure (blue)
- Gules (red)
- Sable (Black)
- Or (gold)
- Vert (green)
- Purpure (purple)
- Argent (silver)

Lines to divide shields

- Invected
- Engrailed
- Indented
- Embattled
- Dovetailed
- Potent
- Nebuly
- Wavy

Metals

Furs

- Ermine
- Vair

Shield designs

- Barry
- Bendy
- Paly
- Chevron
- Chequy
- Lozenge
- Fusil
- Barry-bendy
- Paly-bendy
- Gyronny
- Compony
- Barry per pale

Cadency symbols

- File or Label (oldest son)
- Crescent (second son)
- Mullet (third son)
- Martlet (fourth son)
- Annulet (fifth son)
- Fleur-de-lis (sixth son)
- Rose (seventh son)
- Cross Moline (eighth son)
- Octofoil (ninth son)

Kinds of charges

A charge is a symbol of an object or figure that appears on a shield. Animals are among the most popular charges.

- Swords
- Ship
- Tower
- Unicorn
- Lion
- Dragon
- Arms
- Wolf's head
- Tortoise

Patterns of family relationships

Two or more arms were sometimes combined on one shield in order to show family relationships. The earliest methods of *marshaling,* as this procedure is called, are shown below. The arms of two families are placed side by side or one within the other.

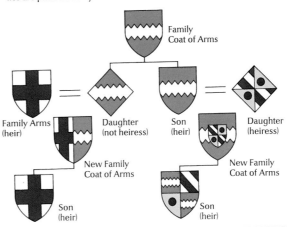

- Family Coat of Arms
- Family Arms (heir)
- Daughter (not heiress)
- Son (heir)
- Daughter (heiress)
- New Family Coat of Arms
- New Family Coat of Arms
- Son (heir)
- Son (heir)

ABOUT THE USE OF A CROSS ON FLAGS

The cross has been used on flags for more than a thousand years—since the early days of the Holy Roman Empire (about A.D. 800). A number of countries indicate their historic link with the Christian faith by showing a cross on their flags. Denmark's flag (above) is an example of a flag using the Scandinavian cross, a straight-armed, off-center cross that dominates the flag with its arms extending to the flag's edges. According to tradition, the Danish flag fell from heaven on June 15, 1219, during a battle against pagans and was understood to indicate divine favor for Christians. The flag of Greece (above right) features a white-on-blue cross in its *canton* (the upper corner of the flag, next to the staff). This flag emerged in the early 1800's as a symbol of Greek resistance to Muslim Ottoman domination and the nation's commitment to Orthodox Christianity. The flag of Tonga (lower right) was adopted in the 1800's and features a cross in its canton to indicate the Christian faith of the Tongan people.

ABOUT THE USE OF THE FLEUR-DE-LIS ON FLAGS

The *fleur-de-lis* (also spelled fleur-de-lys) is a stylized design that represents irises, and it has long been associated with the French monarchy. As an emblem, the fleur-de-lis has been frequently used in *heraldry*. (Heraldry is the study of the symbols and designs used on coats of arms, flags, seals, and badges.) According to one legend, the symbol represents the lily given to Clovis (466?–511), king of the Franks, by an angel. The lily was said to have sprung from the tears shed by Eve as she left the Garden of Eden.

Since ancient times, the fleur-de-lis has been a symbol of purity. It was adopted by the Roman Catholic Church to represent the holiness of the Virgin Mary. One of the earliest uses of the emblem by a French king dates back to 1060, when the royal seal of Philip I (1052–1108) showed him sitting on his throne holding a staff with a fleur-de-lis at the top. A similar staff was shown on the Great Seal of Louis VII (1137–1180). Louis's signet ring also carried a single fleur-de-lis. Louis is thought to be the first monarch to use several golden fleurs-de-lis on a shield of azure, or sky blue. A blue flag with these flowers, however, may have been used even earlier. This blue flag, the banner of French royalty, is known as the France Ancient. In 1376, Charles V (1364–1380) reduced the number of flowers to three, reportedly to honor the Christian Holy Trinity of Father, Son, and Holy Ghost. That flag is known as the France Modern.

Over the years, the design of the fleur-de-lis has been modified by individual artists and the people who chose the emblem for their flags. For example, an artist might show the fleur-de-lis without any feet or with feet that had a special pedestal, or stand (the "feet" section of a fleur-de-lis is any part of the design below the horizontal band).

✸ FLAG DATA ✸

- The fleur-de-lis was used as a symbol of the French monarchy for almost 1,000 years.

- In this French flag above, known as the France Modern, three golden fleurs-de-lis on a blue *field* (background) may symbolize the three members of the Chrisitan Holy Trinity.

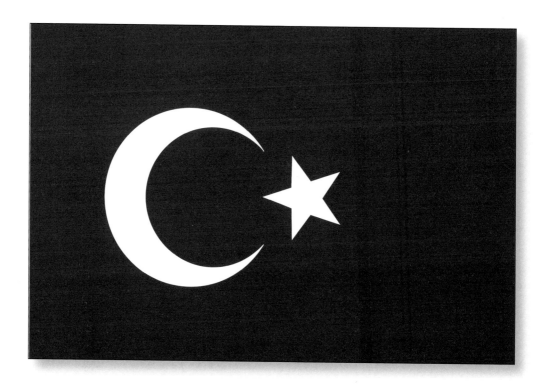

ABOUT THE USE OF THE CRESCENT AND STAR ON FLAGS

Although the crescent and star have come to be regarded as symbols of Islam, their use dates back to ancient times, long before Islam was established. Ancient civilizations throughout the Middle East used a crescent moon as a religious symbol. The ancient city of Byzantium (later Constantinople, now Istanbul) was founded by the Greeks and dedicated to the Greek moon goddess, Artemis. When the emperor Constantine the Great (275?–337) made Christianity the official faith of the Roman Empire in the early A.D. 300's, a star that symbolized Mary, the mother of Jesus Christ, was added to the crescent symbol of the moon goddess.

The crescent and star became associated with Islam when the Muslim peoples of Central Asia captured the Anatolian peninsula (and, eventually, Constantinople) and added the crescent and star of Constantinople to their own plain red flags. Several Turkish flags were used throughout the centuries of the Ottoman Empire, most of them incorporating the crescent and star and the colors red or green. In June 1793, the flag now used as the Turkish national flag was established for that nation's navy, although its star had eight points instead of the current five. The reduction in the number of star points was made about 1844.

The flag of Turkey (above) features the classic crescent and star combination. The eight-pointed star on the flag of Azerbaijan (above right) represents the eight traditional Turkic peoples who live in Central Asia. The crescent on the flag of the Maldives (lower right) indicates the islands' long association with Islam.

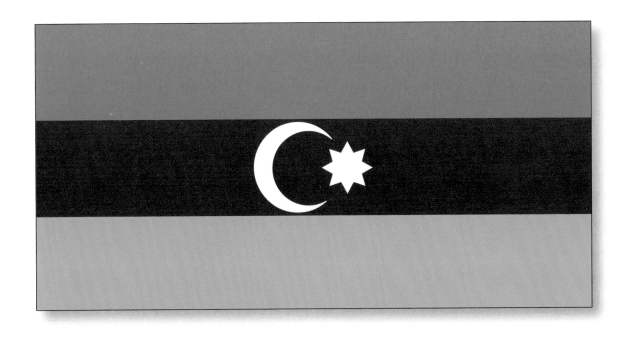

ABOUT THE USE OF THE SUN ON FLAGS

Various symbols of the sun are in use on a number of the world's flags. Antigua (later, Antigua and Barbuda) flew its current flag (above) for the first time on Feb. 27, 1967. The flag's central symbol is a golden sun, representing the sun of a new era.

By contrast, Japanese myths tell that Japan was founded by gods, including the sun goddess Amaterasu. A sun symbol was used in Japan as early as the 1300's, and a popular name for Japan is "Land of the Rising Sun." The current form of Japan's flag (above right), featuring a solid red circle representing the sun, was introduced in 1854 for use on ships and was approved for use on land in 1870, when it became Japan's first national flag.

The sun served as a symbol of the struggle for independence from Spain for many former Spanish colonies in South America, including Argentina and Uruguay. The use of the symbol has been traced to a major public demonstration for independence held in Buenos Aires, Argentina, on May 25, 1810, and it still appears on the flag of Argentina (lower right).

ABOUT THE USE OF ANIMALS ON FLAGS

Some of the world's flags include animals. Albania's flag (above) features a stylized two-headed eagle, a symbol of the Byzantine Empire of which Albania was once a part. Albanians' own name for their land, "Shqipëria," is believed to have emerged during the 16th and 17th centuries. It probably was derived from *shqipe,* or "eagle," which, when modified into *shqipëria,* became "the land of the eagle."

The flag of Kazakhstan (above right) features a yellow steppe eagle in flight, in addition to an image of the sun. Both the sun and the eagle represent the freedom and high ideals of Kazakhstan's people.

Legends tell that Prince Vijaya arrived on the island of Ceylon (now Sri Lanka) from Sinhapura ("Lion City") in India, leading the foundation of the Sinhalese culture on the island in the 400's B.C. Since that time, the Lion Flag (lower right) has been the chief flag of the island's Sinhalese people, the largest ethnic group in the country.

ABOUT THE USE OF STARS ON FLAGS

Many of the world's flags depict stars in various forms. The flag of Australia (above) depicts the Southern Cross, a constellation visible only in the southern hemisphere and featured on many flags of countries of the southern Pacific.

Ghana's flag (above right) features a black five-pointed star, called "the lodestar of African freedom." A lodestar is a star which can be used as a guide for those traveling at night.

The flag of Aruba (lower right) features a red four-pointed star. The red of the star is said to stand for the islanders' love of their country. Other meanings suggested by the star emblem include the island itself—the diversity of its immigrants' origins, its four main languages, the four directions of the wind, and the four points of a compass.

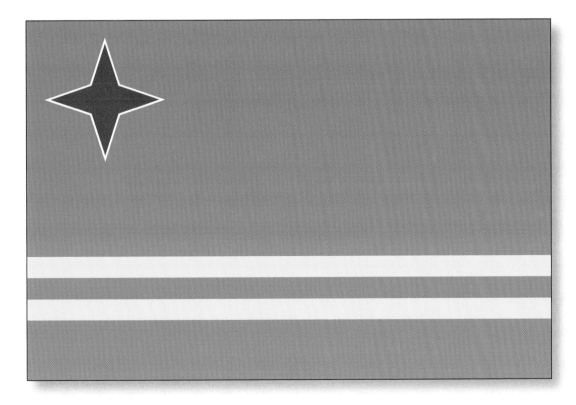

ABOUT THE USE OF TOOLS ON FLAGS

Tools are featured on a number of flags around the world. The flag of Mozambique (above) shows an open book, an assault rifle, and a hoe, which symbolize education, the defense of freedom, and the country's peasant population.

Belize's flag (above right) features two figures holding an ax and a paddle, tools that have been important to Belize's economy. The ax represents the tools used to harvest mahogany trees in Belize's forests, and the paddle represents the boats used to ship timber on Belize's rivers for export. The top left section of the coat of arms shows a paddle and a maul (a long, heavy hammer), and the top right section of the shield shows a two-handed saw and an ax. The bottom section of the shield features a sailing ship.

The flag of the U.S.S.R. (lower right) showed a hammer and sickle in the *canton* (the upper corner of the flag, next to the staff). The hammer symbolized industrial workers and the sickle symbolized agricultural workers.

ABOUT THE USE OF PLANTS ON FLAGS

A number of the flags of the world feature plants on them. The cedar tree has been a symbol of Lebanon for thousands of years because cedars were plentiful throughout Lebanon in ancient times. It remains a potent image of strength and wealth and appears on the country's flag (above).

Equatorial Guinea's flag (above right) shows the country's coat of arms, which features a silk-cotton tree, also called the god tree or kapok tree. The first treaty between a local ruler and Spain was signed under a tree of this type.

Haiti's flag (lower right) has the country's coat of arms at its center, which includes a palm tree with a liberty cap at its top. Palm trees thrive in tropical environments and grow in many parts of Haiti.

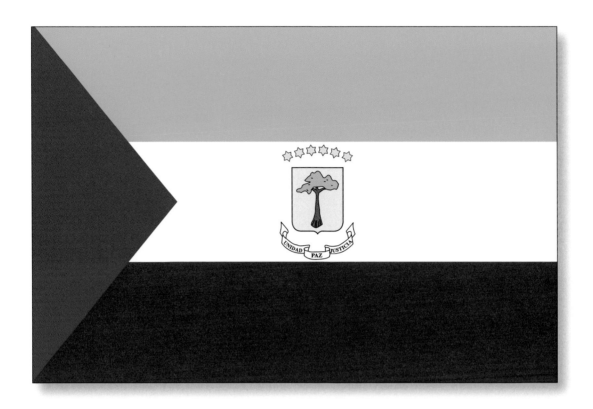

Note: Page references in **bold** indicate volume numbers.

A

Aas, Kari, **12**:27
Abd al-Qadir, **1**:12
Abdullah, ruler of Transjordan, **5**:16
Abolitionists, **5**:40
Aborigines
  of Australia, **1**:24
  of New South Wales, **1**:28
  of South Australia, **1**:34
  of Taiwan, **8**:40
  of Victoria, **1**:38
  of Western Australia, **1**:40
Abraham, **5**:8
Abu Dhabi (United Arab Emirates), **9**:10–**9**:11
Acadians, **2**:42
Addis Ababa (Ethiopia), **12**:8
Afghanistan, flag of, **1**:8–**1**:9
Afonso III, King of Portugal, **7**:24
Afonso Henriques, King of Portugal, **7**:24
AFPFL (Anti-Fascist People's Freedom League), **6**:28
Africa
  African Union flag, **12**:8
  Algeria, **1**:12–**1**:13
  Angola, **1**:16–**1**:17
  Benin, **2**:10–**2**:11
  Botswana, **2**:18–**2**:19
  Burkina Faso, **2**:26–**2**:27
  Burundi, **2**:28–**2**:29
  Cameroon, **2**:32–**2**:33
  Cape Verde, **3**:8–**3**:9
  Central African Republic, **3**:10–**3**:11
  Chad, **3**:12–**3**:13
  Comoros, **3**:24–**3**:25
  Congo (Brazzaville), **3**:26–**3**:27
  Congo (Kinshasa), **3**:28–**3**:29
  Côte d'Ivoire, **3**:32–**3**:33
  Djibouti, **3**:48–**3**:49
  Egypt, **3**:58–**3**:59
  Equatorial Guinea, **3**:62–**3**:63
  Eritrea, **4**:8–**4**:9
  Ethiopia, **4**:12–**4**:13
  Gabon, **4**:22–**4**:23
  Gambia, **4**:24–**4**:25
  Ghana, **4**:30–**4**:31
  Guinea, **4**:38–**4**:39
  Guinea-Bissau, **4**:40–**4**:41
  Kenya, **5**:20–**5**:21
  Lesotho, **5**:38–**5**:39
  Liberia, **5**:40–**5**:41
  Libya, **5**:42–**5**:43
  Madagascar, **5**:52–**5**:53
  Malawi, **5**:54–**5**:55
  Mali, **5**:60–**5**:61
  Mauritania, **6**:10–**6**:11
  Mauritius, **6**:12–**6**:13
  Morocco, **6**:24–**6**:25
  Mozambique, **6**:26–**6**:27
  Namibia, **6**:30–**6**:31
  Niger, **6**:52–**6**:53
  Nigeria, **6**:54–**6**:55
  Rwanda, **7**:40–**7**:41
  São Tomé and Príncipe, **7**:52–**7**:53
  Senegal, **7**:56–**7**:57
  Seychelles, **8**:8–**8**:9
  Sierra Leone, **8**:10–**8**:11
  Somalia, **8**:20–**8**:21
  Somaliland, **12**:31
  South Africa, **8**:22–**8**:23
  Sudan, **8**:28–**8**:29
  Swaziland, **8**:32–**8**:33
  Tanzania, **8**:44–**8**:45
  Togo, **8**:48–**8**:49
  Tunisia, **8**:54–**8**:55
  Uganda, **8**:62–**8**:63
  Western Sahara, **12**:33
  Zambia, **11**:68–**11**:69
  Zimbabwe, **11**:70–**11**:71
Africa Day (African Liberation Day), **12**:8
African Democratic Rally, **2**:32, **5**:60
African National Congress (ANC), **8**:22
African Party for the Independence of Guinea-Bissau and Cape Verde (PAIGC), **3**:8, **4**:40
African Union flag, **12**:8
Afrikaners, **8**:22
Aguinaldo, Emilio, **7**:20
Aitutaki Island, **6**:44
Ajman (United Arab Emirates), **9**:10–**9**:11
Akinkunmi, Michael Taiwo, **6**:54
Aksum Kingdom, **4**:8, **4**:12
Alabama, flag of, **10**:10–**10**:11
Alamo flag, **11**:36
Alamo (TX), **10**:94, **11**:36
Alaska
  flag of, **10**:12–**10**:13
  joins the Union, **11**:53
  Russian-American Company's flag, **11**:23
Alaungpaya, King of Burma (now Myanmar), **6**:28
Albania flag of, **1**:10–**1**:11, **12**:52
Albert, Duke of York, **1**:26
Alberta, flag of, **2**:36–**2**:37
Aleutian Islands (Alaska), **10**:12
Aleuts, **10**:12
Alexander the Great, **5**:36, **5**:50
Al Fujayrah (United Arab Emirates), **9**:10–**9**:11
Algeria, flag of, **1**:12–**1**:13
Algonquian, or Algonguin, Indians
  of Connecticut, **10**:22
  of Delaware, **10**:24
  of Maine, **10**:46
  of Massachusetts, **10**:50
  of New Brunswick, **2**:42
  of New Hampshire, **10**:66
  of New York, **10**:72
  of Rhode Island, **10**:86
Allahu akbar (God is greatest), **4**:56, **4**:58
Allen, Ethan, **10**:98, **11**:28
All-India Muslim League, **7**:8
Alphabet, International Alphabet flags, **12**:38–**12**:39
Al-Sabah family, **5**:28
Al-Thani family, **7**:30
Althing (world's first parliament), **4**:50
Amador Guerrero, Manuel, **7**:12
Amanullah, King of Afghanistan, **1**:8
Amaterasu (sun goddess), **5**:14, **12**:50
Amazon (Greek myth), **10**:100
Amazon River, **2**:20
American Civil War. *See* Civil War, American
American Indians
  of Alabama, **10**:10
  of Arizona, **10**:14
  of Arkansas, **10**:16
  of California, **10**:18
  of Colorado, **10**:20
  of Connecticut, **10**:22
  of Delaware, **10**:24
  of Florida, **10**:26
  of Georgia, **10**:28
  of Idaho, **10**:32
  of Illinois, **10**:34
  of Indiana, **10**:36
  of Iowa, **10**:38
  of Kansas, **10**:40
  of Kentucky, **10**:42
  of Louisiana, **10**:44
  of Maine, **10**:46
  of Maryland, **10**:48
  of Massachusetts, **10**:50
  of Michigan, **10**:52
  of Minnesota, **10**:54
  of Mississippi, **10**:56
  of Missouri, **10**:58
  of Montana, **10**:60
  of Nebraska, **10**:62
  of Nevada, **10**:64
  of New Hampshire, **10**:66
  of New Jersey, **10**:68
  of New Mexico, **10**:70
  of New York, **10**:72
  of North America, **10**:8
  of North Carolina, **10**:74
  of North Dakota, **10**:76
  of Ohio, **10**:78
  of Oklahoma, **10**:80
  of Oregon, **10**:82
  of Pennsylvania, **10**:84
  of Rhode Island, **10**:86
  of South Carolina, **10**:88
  of South Dakota, **10**:90
  of Texas, **10**:94
  of Utah, **10**:96
  of Vermont, **10**:98
  of Virginia, **10**:100
  of Washington, **10**:102
  of Washington, D.C., **10**:104
  of Wyoming, **10**:110
American Legion, **10**:12
American Revolution. *See* Revolutionary War in America; United States, colonial and Revolutionary War flags
American Samoa, **7**:48, **11**:8–**11**:9
Anasazi Indians, **10**:14, **10**:20
Anatolia, **8**:56
ANC (African National Congress), **8**:22

Andes Mountains, **3**:56, **7**:18
Anding, Ida, **10**:90
Andorra, flag of, **1**:14–**1**:15
Andros, Edmund, **11**:25
Andros Flag, **11**:25
Anegada (British Virgin
    Islands), **9**:28
Angel Falls (Venezuela), **11**:62
Angkor (Cambodia), **2**:30
Angkor Wat (Cambodia), **2**:30
Angola, flag of, **1**:16–**1**:17
Anguilla, **7**:42; flag of,
    9:22–**9**:23
Angus, King of Scotland, **9**:18
Animal symbols, **12**:52–**12**:53.
    See also specific animals
Anjouan Island (Comoros),
    3:24
Antarctic Treaty, **12**:28
Antarctica, flag of, **12**:28–**12**:29
Anti-Fascist People's Freedom
    League (AFPFL), **6**:28
Antigua and Barbuda, flag of,
    1:18–**1**:19, **12**:50
Apartheid, **2**:18, **8**:22
Appalachian Ridge, **10**:92
Appenine Mountains, **7**:50
Appomattox (Virginia), **10**:100
Arab League flag, **12**:9
Arab Liberation Flag
    Egypt's flag and, **3**:58
    Sudan's flag and, **8**:28
    Syria's flag and, **8**:38
    Yemen's flag and, **11**:66
Arab Revolt Flag
    Jordan and, **5**:16
    Palestinian Authority's flag,
        12:30
    pan-Arab colors, **12**:36
    Sudan and, **8**:28
    Syria and, **8**:38
    United Arab Emirates' flag
        and, **9**:10
Arabs
    of Algeria, **1**:12
    of Comoros, **3**:24
    control of Kenya, **5**:20
    of Egypt, **3**:58
    of Iraq, **4**:58
    Israel and, **5**:8
    of Jordan, **5**:16
    of Kuwait, **5**:28
    of Lebanon, **5**:36
    of Libya, **5**:42

of Morocco, **6**:24
of Oman, **6**:58
pan-Arab colors, **12**:36
red flag of, **5**:58
of Saudi Arabia, **7**:54
of Sudan, **8**:28
of Syria, **8**:38
of Tanzania, **8**:44
of Tunisia, **8**:54
of United Arab Emirates,
    9:10
of Yemen, **11**:66
Aragon, kingdom of, **8**:24
Araucanian Indians, **3**:14
Arawak Indians
    of Dominica, **3**:50
    of Grenada, **4**:34
    of Guyana, **4**:42
    of Haiti, **4**:44
    of Jamaica, **5**:12
    of Puerto Rico, **11**:14
    of Saint Kitts and Nevis, **7**:42
    of Saint Lucia, **7**:44
    of Saint Vincent and the
        Grenadines, **7**:46
    of Trinidad and Tobago, **8**:52
Arce, Manuel José, **3**:60
Ardennes mountain system,
    5:48
Argentina
    Falkland Islands and, **9**:32
    flag of, **1**:20–**1**:21, **12**:50,
        12:51
Arikora Indians, **10**:90
Arizona, flag of, **10**:14–**10**:15;
    11:52
Arkansas, flag of, **10**:16–**10**:17
Armenia, flag of, **1**:22–**1**:23;
    12:12
Armillary sphere, **7**:24–**7**:25
Armorial flags, **7**:22
Arthur, King, **9**:20
Aruba, flag of, **6**:38–**6**:39, **12**:54,
    12:55
Aryans, **4**:56
Ascension Island, **9**:46
ASEAN (Association of
    Southeast Asian; Nations)
    flag, **12**:10
Ashoka, Emperor of India, **4**:52
Ash Shariqah (United Arab
    Emirates), **9**:10–**9**:11
Asia. *See also* Middle East;
    Southeast Asia

Association of Southeast
    Asian Nations flag, **12**:10
Afghanistan, **1**:8–**1**:9
Armenia, **1**:22–**1**:23
Azerbaijan (Asian),
    1:48–**1**:49
Bahrain, **1**:52–**1**:53
Bangladesh, **1**:54–**1**:55
Bhutan, **2**:12–**2**:13
Brunei, **2**:22–**2**:23
Cambodia, **2**:30–**2**:31
China, **3**:16–**3**:17
Cyprus, **3**:38–**3**:39
East Timor, **3**:54–**3**:55
Egypt (Asian), **3**:58–**3**:59
Georgia (Asian), **4**:26–**4**:27
India, **4**:52–**4**:53
Indonesia (Asian),
    4:54–**4**:55
Iran, **4**:56–**4**:57
Iraq, **4**:58–**4**:59
Israel, **5**:8–**5**:9
Japan, **5**:14–**5**:15
Jordan, **5**:16–**5**:17
Kazakhstan (Asian),
    5:18–**5**:19
Korea, North, **5**:24–**5**:25
Korea, South, **5**:26–**5**:27
Kuwait, **5**:28–**5**:29
Kyrgyzstan, **5**:30–**5**:31
Laos, **5**:32–**5**:33
Lebanon, **5**:36–**5**:37
Malaysia, **5**:56–**5**:57
Maldives, **5**:58–**5**:59
Mongolia, **6**:22–**6**:23
Myanmar, **6**:28–**6**:29
Nepal, **6**:34–**6**:35
Oman, **6**:58–**6**:59
Pakistan, **7**:8–**7**:9
Philippines, **7**:20–**7**:21
Qatar, **7**:30–**7**:31
Russia (Asian), **7**:34–**7**:35
Saudi Arabia, **7**:54–**7**:55
Singapore, **8**:12–**8**:13
Sri Lanka, **8**:26–**8**:27
Syria, **8**:38–**8**:39
Taiwan, **8**:40–**8**:41
Tajikistan, **8**:42–**8**:43
Thailand, **8**:46–**8**:47
Turkey (Asian), **8**:56–**8**:57
Turkmenistan, **8**:58–**8**:59
United Arab Emirates,
    9:10–**9**:11
Uzbekistan, **11**:56–**11**:57

Vietnam, **11**:64–**11**:65
Yemen, **11**:66–**11**:67
Asia Minor, **8**:56
Association of Southeast Asian
    Nations (ASEAN) flag,
    12:10
Atafu Island (Tokelau), **6**:49
Atiu Island (Cook Islands), **6**:44
Atlantic Coastal Plain, **10**:48
Atlas Mountains, **6**:24
Atuagagdliutit (newspaper), **3**:46
Aury, Luis, **4**:36
Austral island group, **4**:20
Australasian Anti-Transportation
    League, **1**:38
Australasian United Steam
    Navigation Company, **8**:8
Australia
    Australian Capital Territory,
        1:26–**1**:27
    Christmas Island, **1**:42–**1**:43
    Commonwealth of Nations
        flag, **12**:13
    flag of, **1**:24–**1**:25, **12**:54
    Nauru and, **6**:32
    New South Wales, **1**:28–**1**:29
    Norfolk Island, **1**:44–**1**:45
    Northern Territory,
        1:30–**1**:31
    Papua New Guinea and, **7**:14
    Queensland, **1**:32–**1**:33
    South Australia, **1**:34–**1**:35
    Tasmania, **1**:36–**1**:37
    Victoria, **1**:38–**1**:39
    Western Australia, **1**:40–**1**:41
Australian Blue Ensign, **1**:24
Australian Capital Territory,
    flag of, **1**:26–**1**:27
Australian Federation Flag, **1**:24
Austria
    Belgium and, **1**:60
    flag of, **1**:46–**1**:47
    Hungary and, **4**:48
    rule of Poland, **7**:22
Awami League, **1**:54
Axis powers, **3**:34
Azerbaijan
    Commonwealth of
        Independent States flag,
        12:12
    flag of, **1**:48–**1**:49, **12**:48,
        12:49
Azoreans, **7**:26
Azores, flag of, **7**:26–**7**:27

Azores Liberation Front, **7**:26
Aztec Indians, **6**:14

B

Baath Party, **4**:58
Baden-Powell, Robert, **12**:26
Badge
  of Anguilla, **9**:22
  of Bahamas, **1**:50
  of Barbadian ensign, **1**:56
  British Blue Ensign and, **9**:52
  definition of, *See* page 6 of
    any volume
  of Dominica, **3**:50
  of Fiji, **4**:14
  of Gambia, **4**:24
  of Gibraltar, **9**:34
  of Hong Kong, **3**:18
  of New South Wales, **1**:28
  of Queensland flag, **1**:32
  of Saint Helena, **9**:46
  of Sierra Leone, **8**:10
  of Solomon Islands, **8**:18
  of South Australia, **1**:34
  of Straits Settlements, **8**:12
  of Tasmania, **1**:36
  of Trinidad, **8**:52
  of Turks and Caicos Islands,
    9:50–**9**:51
  of Uganda, **8**:62
  of Victoria, **1**:38
Badlands (North Dakota), **10**:76
Badlands (South Dakota), **10**:90
Baffin Island, **2**:50
Bahamas, flag of, **1**:50–**1**:51
Bahrain, flag of, **1**:52–**1**:53
Baltic islands (Estonia), **4**:10
Baltimore, Lords, **10**:48
Baltimore (Maryland), **10**:48
Baluchis, **6**:58
Bangladesh, flag of, **1**:54–**1**:55
Banjul (Gambia), **4**:24
Banner of arms, **9**:16
Banner of Victory, **9**:14
Bantu-speaking ethnic groups,
  6:26, **8**:44
Barbados, flag of, **1**:56–**1**:57
Barbary ape, **9**:34
Barnet, James, **1**:28
Bartram, Graham, **12**:28
Basin and Range Region
  (Arizona), **10**:14
Basin and Range Region
  (Idaho), **10**:32

Basotho, **5**:38
Basotho National Party, **5**:38
Basutoland, **5**:38
BAT (British Antarctic
  Territories), **9**:48
Batavian Republic, **6**:36
Battle of Bennington, **11**:44
Battle of Boyacá, **3**:22
Battle of Bull Run, **11**:41
Battle of Carillon, **2**:56
Battle of Concord, **11**:24
Battle of Cowpens, **11**:47
Battle of Hastings, **9**:20
Battle of Lake Erie, **11**:35
Battle of Lexington, **11**:24, **11**:31
Battle of Lyndanisse, **3**:42
Battle of Manassas, **11**:41
Bauhinia flower, **3**:18–**3**:19
Bavarian dynasty, **4**:32
Bayeux Tapestry, **9**:36
Beanlands, Arthur John, **2**:38
Bear, **10**:58, **10**:59
Bear Flag, **10**:18, **11**:38
Bear Flag Revolt, **10**:18
Beatriz, of Castile, **7**:24, **7**:26
Bebek, Zvonimir, **2**:16
Beddoe, Alan B., **2**:42, **2**:46, **2**:60
Bedford Flag, **11**:24
Belarus, flag of, **1**:58–**1**:59; **12**:12
Belgian Congo, **3**:28
Belgium
  Burundi and, **2**:28
  Congo (Kinshasa) ruled by,
    3:28
  flag of, **1**:60–**1**:61
  rule of Rwanda, **7**:40
Belize, flag of, **2**:8–**2**:9, **12**:56,
  12:57
Bengal, **1**:54
Benin, flag of, **2**:10–**2**:11
Bennington Flag, **11**:44
Benson, Benny, **10**:12
Berbers, **1**:12, **5**:42, **6**:24
Bermuda, flag of, **9**:24–**9**:25
Bermudez, Juan de, **9**:24
Bessant, Robert, **2**:46
Bhutan, flag of, **2**:12–**2**:13
Bible, **5**:8, **10**:22
BIOT (British Indian Ocean
  Territory), flag of,
  9:26–**9**:27
Bird of paradise, **7**:14–**7**:15
Bison, **10**:110, **10**:111
Blackfoot Indian nation, **2**:36

Black Hills (South Dakota),
  10:90
Black Sea, **4**:26
Bligh, William, **1**:44
Bluegrass Region (Kentucky),
  10:42
Blue Ridge mountain range,
  10:92
Bo tree, **8**:26
Boers, **8**:22
Boganda, Barthélemy, **3**:10
Bogotá (Colombia), **3**:22
Bohemia, **3**:40
Bokassa, Jean Bédel, **3**:10
Bolívar, Simón, **2**:14, **3**:22
Bolivia, flag of, **2**:14–**2**:15
Bolsheviks, **7**:38. *See also*
  Communism
Bonaire Island, **6**:40
Bonaparte, Napoleon, **4**:28, **9**:46
Bonnie Blue Flag, **10**:56, **11**:39
Boone, Daniel, **10**:92
Borinquen Indians, **11**:14
Borneo island, **5**:56
Bosnia-Herzegovina, flag of,
  2:16–**2**:17
Bosporus, **8**:56
Botswana, flag of, **2**:18–**2**:19
Bounty (ship), **1**:44, **9**:44
Bourbons, **4**:18, **8**:24
Boy Scouts flag, **12**:26
Brady Guard, **10**:52
Brattleboro (Vermont), **10**:98
Brazil, flag of, **2**:20–**2**:21
British Antarctic Survey, **9**:48
British Antarctic Territories
  (BAT), **9**:48
British Blue Ensign
  Anguilla's flag, **9**:22
  British Red Ensign and, **9**:54
  British Virgin Islands' flag,
    9:28
  Cayman Islands and, **9**:30
  Falkland Islands' flag, **9**:32
  Gambia's flag and, **4**:24
  Gibraltar and, **9**:34
  Hong Kong's flag with, **3**:18
  information about,
    9:52–**9**:53
  Montserrat's flag, **9**:42–**9**:43
  New Zealand flag, **6**:42
  Pitcairn Islands Group flag,
    9:44
  Saint Helena's flag, **9**:46–**9**:47

Sierra Leone and, **8**:10
Solomon Islands and, **8**:18
South Georgia and South
  Sandwich Islands, **9**:48
Straits Settlements and, **8**:12
Trinidad and Tobago, **8**:52
Turks and Caicos Islands'
  flag, **9**:50–**9**:51
Union Jack on, **9**:12
British Columbia, flag of,
  2:38–**2**:39
British crown dependency
  Isle of Man, **9**:40–**9**:41
  Jersey, **9**:38–**9**:39
British Guiana, **4**:42
British Indian Ocean Territory
  (BIOT), flag of, **9**:26–**9**:27
British Isles, **9**:12
British Red Ensign
  Bermuda's flag, **9**:24
  British Blue Ensign and, **9**:52
  British Virgin Islands and,
    9:28
  Cayman Islands and, **9**:30
  Falkland Islands and, **9**:32
  Gibraltar and, **9**:34
  information about,
    9:54–**9**:55
  Isle of Man and, **9**:40
  New Zealand flag, **6**:42
  Palestine's flag, **12**:30
  Turks and Caicos Islands'
    flag, **9**:50
  Union Jack on, **9**:12
British Royal Air Force, **11**:70
British Union Flag
  on Continental Colors flag,
    11:45
  English settlement flag,
    11:20
  Taunton Flag and, **11**:27
British Virgin Islands, flag of,
  9:28–**9**:29
British White Ensign
  British Blue Ensign and, **9**:52
  British Red Ensign and, **9**:54
  Union Jack on, **9**:12
Bronck, Jonas, **10**:72
Brownell, Frederick, **8**:22
Brunei, flag of, **2**:22–**2**:23
Budapest (Hungary), **4**:48
Buddha (Enlightened One),
  8:26
Buddhism, **4**:52, **6**:22, **8**:26

Buenos Aires (Argentina), **1**:20
Buganda, kingdom of, **8**:62
Bulgaria, flag of, **2**:24–**2**:25
Bunyoro-Kitara, kingdom of, **8**:62
Burgoyne, John, **11**:44
Burkina Faso, flag of, **2**:26–**2**:27
Burma. *See* Myanmar
Burnet, David, **11**:37
Burundi, flag of, **2**:28–**2**:29
Byelorussian Soviet Socialist Republic, flag of, **1**:58
Byzantine Empire, **1**:10, **8**:14
Byzantium, **8**:56, **12**:48

C
Cabral, Gonzalo, **7**:26
Cadwaladr, Prince, **9**:20
Caicos and Turks Islands, flag of, **9**:50–**9**:51
Cajuns, **10**:44
Cakobau, Fijian chief, **4**:14
California, flag of, **10**:18–**10**:19; **11**:38
California grizzly bear, **10**:18, **10**:19
California Republic flag, **10**:18–**10**:19, **11**:38
Calligraphy, **7**:54
Calpe, Mount, **9**:34
Calvert family, **10**:48
Calvert, Leonard, **10**:48
Cambodia, flag of, **2**:30–**2**:31
Cambrian Mountains, **9**:20
Cameroon, flag of, **2**:32–**2**:33
Canada
    Alberta, **2**:36–**2**:37
    badge on British Red Ensign, **9**:24
    British Columbia, **2**:38–**2**:39
    Commonwealth of Nations flag, **12**:13
    flag of, **2**:34–**2**:35
    Manitoba, **2**:40–**2**:41
    New Brunswick, **2**:42–**2**:43
    Newfoundland and Labrador, **2**:44–**2**:45
    Northwest Territories, **2**:46–**2**:47
    Nova Scotia, **2**:48–**2**:49
    Nunavut, **2**:50–**2**:51
    Ontario, **2**:52–**2**:53
    Prince Edward Island, **2**:54–**2**:55

    Quebec, **2**:56–**2**:57
    Saskatchewan, **2**:58–**2**:59
    Yukon, **2**:60–**2**:61
Canadian pale, **2**:60
Canadian Red Ensign
    Manitoba's flag, **2**:40
    Ontario's flag, **2**:52
    use of, **2**:34
Canadian Shield, **2**:46, **2**:56
Canberra (Australian Capital Territory), **1**:26
Canton
    definition of, *See* page 6 of any volume
    geographical meaning of, **8**:36
Canty, Brian, **9**:22
Cape Breton Island, **2**:48
Cape Verde, flags of, **3**:8–**3**:9; **4**:40
Carib Indians
    of Anguilla, **9**:22
    of British Virgin Islands, **9**:28
    of Costa Rica, **3**:30
    of Dominica, **3**:50
    of Grenada, **4**:34
    of Guyana, **4**:42
    of Saint Kitts and Nevis, **7**:42
    of Saint Lucia, **7**:44
    of Saint Vincent and the Grenadines, **7**:46
    of Trinidad and Tobago, **8**:52
    of Virgin Islands of the United States, **11**:16
Caribbean Community and Common Market (CARICOM) flag, **12**:11
Carillon Flag, **2**:57
Carillon-Sacre Coeur, **2**:57
Caroline Island group, **6**:16
Carolinians, **6**:16, **11**:12
Carpathian Mountains, **7**:32
Carpets, **8**:58
Carriacou (Grenada), **4**:34
Carthage (Tunisia), **8**:54
Cartier, Jacques, **2**:56
Cascade Range, **10**:82, **10**:102
Casimir the Great, King of Poland, **7**:22
Castile
    Azores flag and, **7**:26
    Castile and León, banner of, **11**:18
    Portugal's flag and, **7**:24

Castro, Fidel, **3**:36
Catalonia (Spain), **8**:24
Cayman Brac (Cayman Islands), **9**:30
Cayman Islands, flag of, **9**:30–**9**:31
Ceausescu, Nicolae, **7**:32
Cedar tree, **5**:36, **5**:37
Celje, **8**:16
Celts, **4**:60, **9**:20, **9**:40
Center, Mrs. Edward H., **10**:54
Central African Republic, flag of, **3**:10–**3**:11
Central America
    Belize, **2**:8–**2**:9
    Costa Rica, **3**:30–**3**:31
    El Salvador, **3**:60–**3**:61
    Guatemala, **4**:36–**4**:37
    Honduras, **4**:46–**4**:47
    Nicaragua, **6**:50–**6**:51
    Panama, **7**:12–**7**:13
Central Lowlands (Scotland), **9**:18
Cesta Tower (San Marino), **7**:50
Ceylon. *See* Sri Lanka
Chad, flag of, **3**:12–**3**:13
Chagos Archipelago island group, **9**:26
Chakra, **8**:46
Chakri dynasty, **8**:46
Chamorros, **11**:10, **11**:12
Channel Islands
    Guernsey, flag of, **9**:36–**9**:37
    Jersey, flag of, **9**:38–**9**:39
Charlemagne, King of the Franks, **1**:14, **5**:44, **8**:24
Charles III, King of Spain, **8**:24
Charles IV, Grand Duke of Luxembourg, **5**:48
Charleston Harbor (South Carolina), **10**:88, **11**:33
Charles V, King of France, **12**:46
Charles V, King of Spain, **5**:62
Chesapeake (battleship), **11**:35
Chesapeake Bay, **10**:48
Cheyenne Indians, **10**:90
Chiang Kai-shek, **8**:40
Chile, flag of, **3**:14–**3**:15
China
    flag of, **3**:16–**3**:17
    Hong Kong, **3**:18–**3**:19
    Macao, **3**:20–**3**:21
    Mongolia and, **6**:22

rule of Vietnam, **11**:64
Taiwan and, **8**:40
Chinese, **8**:12, **8**:40
Christian, Fletcher, **9**:44
Christianity
    in Armenia, **1**:22
    crescent and star symbols and, **12**:48
    cross symbol and, **12**:44–**12**:45
    England's flag and, **9**:14
    in Jamaica, **5**:12
    in Northern Ireland, **9**:16
    Order of Christ, **7**:28
    in Tonga, **8**:50
    Turkey's flag and, **8**:56
Christiansen, Thue, **3**:46
Christmas Island, **1**:42–**1**:43
Church of Jesus Christ of Latter-day Saints (Mormons), **10**:96
Church of St. George, **9**:14
Cimmerians, **7**:34
Cinchona tree, **7**:18, **7**:19
CIS (Commonwealth of Independent States) flag, **12**:12
Cispadine Republic, **5**:10
Civil ensign, **1**:50
Civil Rights Movement, **10**:10, **10**:16
Civil War, American
    Alabama in, **10**:10
    Arkansas in, **10**:16
    Bonnie Blue Flag, **11**:39
    Confederate Battle Flag, **11**:41
    Confederate Flag, **11**:43
    Connecticut's flag and, **10**:22
    Florida in, **10**:26
    Georgia in, **10**:28
    Honduran flag and, **4**:46
    Louisiana and, **10**:44
    Maryland in, **10**:48
    Mississippi's flag and, **10**:56
    Missouri and, **10**:58
    Nevada and, **10**:64
    North Carolina in, **10**:74
    South Carolina in, **10**:88
    Stainless Banner, **11**:42
    Stars and Bars flag, **11**:40
    U.S. flag of 1859 to 1861, **11**:49
    Virginia in, **10**:100
    West Virginia and, **10**:106

Clark, William, **10**:32
Clovis, King of the Franks,
      12:46
Coat of arms
   of Alabama, **10**:10
   of Alberta, **2**:36, **2**:37
   of Antigua and Barbuda flag,
      1:18
   of Australian Capital
      Territory, **1**:26
   of Austria, **1**:46
   of Basotho, **5**:38
   of Belgium, **1**:60
   of Belize, **2**:8
   of Bermuda, **9**:24, **9**:25
   of Bolivia, **2**:14, **2**:15
   of Bosnia-Herzegovina, **2**:16
   of Brazil, **2**:20
   of British Indian Ocean
      Territory, **9**:26, **9**:27
   of British Virgin Islands,
      9:28, **9**:29
   of Brunei, **2**:22, **2**:23
   of Bulgaria, **2**:24
   of Burkina Faso, **2**:26
   of Calvert family, **10**:48
   of Canada, **2**:34
   of Cayman Islands, **9**:30,
      9:31
   of Connecticut, **10**:22, **10**:23
   of Costa Rica, **3**:30, **3**:31
   of Croatia, **3**:34
   of Czech Republic, **3**:40
   of Delaware, **10**:24–**10**:25
   of Dominica, **3**:50
   of Dominican Republic,
      3:52–**3**:53
   of Ecuador, **3**:56–**3**:57
   of El Salvador, **3**:60–**3**:61
   of Equatorial Guinea, **3**:62,
      3:63
   of Ethiopia, **4**:12
   of Falkland Islands, **9**:32,
      9:33
   of Faroe Islands, **3**:44
   of Fiji, **4**:14, **4**:15
   of Finland, **4**:16
   of France, **4**:18
   of George Washington,
      10:104
   of Georgia, **10**:28–**10**:29
   of Gibraltar, **9**:34–**9**:35
   of Guatemala, **4**:36
   of Haiti, **4**:44, **4**:45

heraldry of flags, *See* page 7
      of any volume
   of Honduras, **4**:46
   of Hong Kong, **3**:18
   of Hungary, **4**:48
   of Iran, **4**:56–**4**:57
   of Isle of Man, **9**:40
   of Jamaica, **5**:12
   of Jersey, **9**:38, **9**:39
   of Kiribati, **5**:22
   of Macao, **3**:20
   of Maine, **10**:46–**10**:47
   of Malawi, **5**:54
   of Malta, **5**:62
   of Manitoba, **2**:40, **2**:41
   of Massachusetts,
      10:50–**10**:51
   of Mexican flag, **6**:14, **6**:15
   of Michigan, **10**:52–**10**:53
   of Moldova, **6**:18–**6**:19
   of Monaco, **6**:20
   of New Brunswick, **2**:42
   of New Jersey, **10**:68–**10**:69
   of New York, **10**:72, **10**:73
   of Nicaragua, **6**:50
   of North Dakota,
      10:76–**10**:77
   of Northwest Territories,
      2:46
   of Nova Scotia, **2**:48
   of Ontario, **2**:52
   of Papal States, **11**:60–**11**:61
   of Paraguay, **7**:16
   of Pennsylvania, **10**:84–**10**:85
   of Peru, **7**:18–**7**:19
   of Pitcairn Islands Group,
      9:44, **9**:45
   of Poland, **7**:22
   of Portugal, **7**:24–**7**:25
   of Prince Edward Island,
      2:54
   of Rhode Island,
      10:86–**10**:87
   of Saint Helena's flag,
      9:46–**9**:47
   of Saint Lucia, **7**:44
   of Saint Vincent and the
      Grenadines, **7**:46
   of San Marino, **7**:50, **7**:51
   of Saskatchewan, **2**:58
   of Scotland, **9**:18
   of Sierra Leone, **8**:10
   of Singapore, **8**:12
   of Slovakia, **8**:14, **8**:15

   of Slovenia, **8**:16
   of South Georgia and South
      Sandwich Islands,
      9:48–**9**:49
   of Spain, **8**:24, **8**:25
   of Sweden, **8**:34
   of Turks and Caicos Islands'
      flag, **9**:50–**9**:51
   of Tuvalu, **8**:60
   of Uganda, **8**:62
   of Ulster, **9**:16
   of Venezuela, **11**:62–**11**:63
   of Vermont, **10**:98–**10**:99
   of West Virginia,
      10:106–**10**:107
   of Wisconsin, **10**:108–**10**:109
   of Yukon, **2**:60
   of Zambia, **11**:68
   of Zimbabwe, **11**:70
College of Arms (London,
      England), **2**:36, **2**:54
Coloane island, **3**:20
Colombia
   control of Panama, **7**:12
   flag of, **3**:22–**3**:23
   flag of Ecuador and, **3**:56
Colonial Defence Act of 1865,
      9:52
Colonial flags. *See* United
      States, colonial and
      Revolutionary War flags
Colonial Naval Defence Act,
      4:24
Colony and Protectorate of
      Nigeria, **6**:54
Color bars, key to, *See* page 7 of
      any volume
Colorado, flag of, **10**:20–**10**:21
Colorado Plateau, **10**:14
Colorado River, **10**:20
Columbia Plateau, **10**:32
Columbine flower, **10**:20
Columbus, Christopher
   in Antigua and Barbuda,
      1:18
   banner of Castile and León,
      11:18
   British Virgin Islands and,
      9:28
   Cuba and, **3**:36
   Dominica named by, **3**:50
   Dominican Republic and,
      3:52
   Hispaniola named by, **4**:44

   Jamaica and, **5**:12
   Montserrat and, **9**:42
   Puerto Rico and, **11**:14
   Trinidad and Tobago and,
      8:52
   Venezuela and, **11**:62
   Virgin Islands of the United
      States and, **11**:16
Commonwealth of
      Independent States (CIS)
      flag, **12**:12
Commonwealth of Nations
      flag, **12**:13
Communism
   Belarus and, **1**:58
   in Bulgaria, **2**:24
   in Cambodia, **2**:30
   in China, **8**:40
   China's flag and, **3**:16
   in Croatia, **3**:34
   in Cuba, **3**:36
   in Czech Republic, **3**:40
   flag of Hungary and, **4**:48
   Kyrgyzstan and, **5**:30
   in Laos, **5**:32
   in Mongolia, **6**:22
   in North Korea, **5**:24
   in Poland, **7**:22
   red flag of Communists, **4**:28
   in Romania, **7**:32
   in Russia, **7**:34
   in Slovakia, **8**:14
   in Slovenia, **8**:16
   in Tajikistan, **8**:42
   Union of Soviet Socialist
      Republics, **7**:38–**7**:39
   in Uzbekistan, **11**:56
   Vietnam and, **11**:64
   in Yugoslavia, **7**:58
Comoros, flag of, **3**:24–**3**:25
Confederate Battle Flag
   Alabama's flag and, **10**:10
   on Confederate Flag, **11**:43
   Georgia's flag and, **10**:28
   information about, **11**:41
   on Mississippi's flag,
      10:56–**10**:57
   on Stainless Banner, **11**:42
Confederate Flag, **11**:43
Confederate Stars and Bars flag
   Georgia's flag and, **10**:28
   information about, **11**:40
   North Carolina's flag and,
      10:74

Confederate States of America
    Arkansas, **10**:16
    Confederate Battle Flag,
        11:41
    Confederate Flag, **11**:43
    Florida's flag and, **10**:26
    Missouri and, **10**:58
    Stainless Banner, **11**:42
    Stars and Bars flag, **11**:40
Confucius, **3**:16
Congo (Brazzaville), flag of,
    3:26–**3**:27
Congo Free State, **3**:28
Congo (Kinshasa), flag of,
    3:28–**3**:29
Congo-Ubangi river system,
    3:26
Congress of Vienna, **5**:48
Connecticut, flag of,
    10:22–**10**:23
Connecticut River, **10**:22
Conquering Lion of Judah, **4**:12
Constantine I, the Great,
    Roman emperor, **8**:56,
    12:48
Constantinople, **12**:48
Constitutional Convention,
    10:84
Continental Colors flag, **11**:45
Continental Colors (of U.S.),
    10:8
Continental Congress, **10**:8,
    11:45, **11**:46
Convention People's Party, **4**:30
Cook Islands, flag of, **6**:44–**6**:45
Cook, James
    Cook Islands and, **6**:44
    Hawaii visit by, **10**:30
    New South Wales and, **1**:28
    in New Zealand, **6**:42
    Niue and, **6**:46
    Norfolk Island and, **1**:44
    South Georgia Island and,
        9:48
Costa Rica, flag of, **3**:30–**3**:31
Côte d'Ivoire, flag of, **3**:32–**3**:33
Coubertin, Pierre de, **12**:20
Council of Europe, **12**:14
Courtesy flag, **9**:50
Craig, Robert, **1**:34
Crane, crested, **8**:62
Creoles, **7**:52, **8**:30, **10**:44
Crescent
    on Arab League flag, **12**:9

on Missouri's flag, **10**:58
on Pakistan's flag, **7**:8–**7**:9
Red Crescent flag, **12**:16,
    12:17
on Singapore's flag, **8**:12,
    8:13
on Tunisia's flag, **8**:54, **8**:55
on Turkey's flag, **8**:56, **8**:57
on Turkmenistan's flag, **8**:58,
    8:59
on Uzbekistan's flag,
    11:56–**11**:57
Crescent and star symbol,
    12:48–**12**:49
Crested crane, **8**:62
Crete (Greece), **4**:32
Crimean Peninsula, **9**:8
Croatia, flag of, **3**:34–**3**:35
Croats, **2**:16, **3**:34
Cromwell, Oliver, **9**:18
Cross
    International Red Cross flag,
        12:16
    on Slovakia's flag, **8**:14, **8**:15
    on Switzerland's flag,
        8:36–**8**:37
    on Tonga's flag, **8**:50, **8**:51
    use of symbol, **12**:44–**12**:45
Crossland family, **10**:48
Cross of St. Andrew
    on British flag, **9**:12
    British Union Flag, **11**:20
    Confederate Battle Flag,
        11:41
    on Nova Scotia's flag, **2**:48
    on Scotland's flag, **9**:18–**9**:19
Cross of St. George
    on Alberta's flag, **2**:36
    on British Blue Ensign, **9**:52,
        9:53
    on British flag, **9**:12
    on British Red Ensign,
        9:54–**9**:55
    British Union Flag, **11**:20
    England's flag, **9**:14–**9**:15
    on Fiji's coat of arms, **4**:14
    on Guernsey's flag,
        9:36–**9**:37
    heraldry, **12**:42
    on Manitoba's flag, **2**:40, **2**:41
    on Northern Ireland's flag,
        9:16, **9**:17
    on Ontario's flag, **2**:52
    Union Jack and, **9**:18

Cross of St. Patrick
    on British flag, **9**:12
    on Ireland's flag, **4**:60
    on Jersey's flag, **9**:38, **9**:39
Cross of the Order of Christ,
    7:28–**7**:29
Crusades, **9**:14
Cuba, flag of, **3**:36–**3**:37; **11**:14
Cuban Revolutionary Party,
    11:14
Curaçao Island, **6**:40
Cyprus, flag of, **3**:38–**3**:39;
    12:32
Cyrenaica (Libya), **5**:42
Czech Republic, flag of,
    3:40–**3**:41
Czechoslovakia, **3**:40, **8**:14

D
Dacians, **7**:32
Dahomey, kingdom of, **2**:10
Dalmau, Micaela, **11**:14
Damara people, **6**:30
Daughters of the American
    Revolution
    Arkansas flag and, **10**:16
    Illinois flag and, **10**:34
    Indiana flag and, **10**:36
    Iowa flag and, **10**:38
    Missouri flag and, **10**:58
    New Mexico flag and, **10**:70
    Utah flag and, **10**:96
    Washington flag and,
        10:102
    Washington, D.C., flag and,
        10:104
    Wyoming flag and, **10**:110
Day, Harry, **10**:64
Debar, Joseph H. D., **10**:106
De Burgh family, **9**:16
Declaration of Independence,
    10:84
Defaced, **9**:52
Delaware, flag of, **10**:24–**10**:25
Delaware Bay, **10**:24
De La Warr, Lord (governor of
    Virginia), **10**:24
Delta (Mississippi), **10**:56
Democratic Kampuchea, **2**:30
Democratic National Union of
    Mozambique (Udenamo),
    6:26
Democratic Party of Guinea,
    4:38

Democratic People's Republic
    of Korea, **5**:24
Denakil Depression (Ethiopia),
    4:12
Denmark
    Faroe Islands, **3**:44–**3**:45
    flag of, **3**:42–**3**:43
    flag, use of cross, **12**:44
    Greenland, **3**:46–**3**:47
    Iceland and, **4**:50
    rule of Norway, **6**:56
    Sweden and, **8**:34
    Virgin Islands of the United
        States and, **11**:16
Desire (ship), **9**:32
Dharma Chakra ("Wheel of
    Law"), **4**:52
Diana, moon goddess, **8**:56
Diego Garcia island (British
    Indian Ocean Territory),
    9:26
Discovery and settlement flags
    Dutch, **11**:21
    English, **11**:20
    French, **11**:19
    Russian-American
        Company, **11**:23
    Spanish, **11**:18
    Swedish, **11**:22
Djibouti, flag of, **3**:48–**3**:49
Dodson, Sarah, **10**:94
Dogon people, **5**:60
Dominica, flag of, **3**:50–**3**:51
Dominican Republic, flag of,
    3:52–**3**:53
Dominion of New England,
    11:25
Dragon, **2**:12, **2**:13
Dragon flag, **9**:20–**9**:21
Drake, Anthony, **2**:58
Duarte, Juan Pablo, **3**:52
Duarte Peak (Dominican
    Republic), **3**:52
Dubayy (United Arab
    Emirates), **9**:10–**9**:11
Dunant, Jean Henri, **12**:16
Dunn, Charles, **10**:104
Duplessis, Maurice, **2**:56
Dutch
    Aruba and, **6**:38
    control of Suriname, **8**:30
    discovery/settlement flag of,
        11:21
    Netherlands, **6**:36

Netherlands Antilles and, 6:40

in South Africa, 8:22

in Swaziland, 8:32

Dutch West Indies. *See* Netherlands Antilles

Duvalier, François (Papa Doc), 4:44

Duvalier, Jean-Claude (Baby Doc), 4:44

E

Eagle

on American Samoa's flag, 11:8, 11:9

animal symbols on flags, 12:52–12:53

on Austrian flag, 1:46, 1:47

on Illinois flag, 10:34–10:35

on Iowa's flag, 10:38, 10:39

on Kazakhstan's flag, 5:18–5:19, 12:53

on Michigan's flag, 10:52

on North Dakota's flag, 10:77

on Russian-American Company's flag, 11:23

on Russian imperial flag, 7:36, 7:37

on Virgin Islands of the United States flag, 11:16–11:17

on Zambia's flag, 11:68, 11:69

Earthquake, 3:14

East Caicos Island (Turks and Caicos Islands), 9:50

East Falkland Island, 9:32

East Pakistan, 1:54

East Timor, flag of, 3:54–3:55

Easter Rising, 1916, 4:60

Ebeye Island (Marshall Islands), 6:8

EC (European Community), 12:14

Ecuador, flag of, 3:56–3:57

Edward, prince of Great Britain, 2:54

Edward I, King of England, 9:14

Edwards, Harry, 10:96

Egypt

control of Sudan, 8:28

flag of, 3:58–3:59

Libya and, 5:42

in United Arab Republic, 8:38

Eisenmann, John, 10:78

Elephant flag, 8:46

Elizabeth I, Queen of England, 9:14

Elizabeth II, Queen of the United Kingdom

British Indian Ocean Territory coat of arms, 9:26

Jersey flag, 9:38

Ontario's flag and, 2:52

Pitcairn Islands Group coat of arms, 9:44

South Georgia and South Sandwich Islands' coat of arms, 9:48

Tuvalu's flag and, 8:60

Uganda's flag and, 8:62

Ellesmere Island, 2:50

Ellice Islands, 5:22, 8:60

Elliott, Jane, 11:34

Elmer, C. A., 10:32

El Salvador, flag of, 3:60–3:61

Emblem, 12:42. *See also* Coat of arms

England. *See also* Great Britain; United Kingdom

Andros Flag, 11:25

Anguilla and, 9:22

British Blue Ensign, 9:52–9:53

British Red Ensign, 9:54–9:55

discovery/settlement flag of, 11:20

Falkland Islands, 9:32

flag of, 9:14–9:15

Florida and, 10:26

French and Indian Wars, 2:57

Guernsey, 9:36

Scotland and, 9:18

United Kingdom's flag, 9:12–9:13

Wales and, 9:20

Enriquillo, Lake, 3:52

Ensign

British Blue Ensign, 9:52–9:53

British Red Ensign, 9:54–9:55

of Newfoundland and Labrador, 2:44

EPLF (Eritrean People's Liberation Front), 4:8

Equatorial Guinea, flag of, 3:62–3:63, 12:58, 12:59

Eric the Red (Norse explorer), 3:46

Erie, Lake, 10:78

Eritrea, flag of, 4:8–4:9

Eritrean People's Liberation Front (EPLF), 4:8

España, José María, 11:62

Estonia, flag of, 4:10–4:11

Ethiopia

Eritrea and, 4:8

flag of, 4:12–4:13

Organization of African Unity founded in, 12:8

pan-African colors and, 12:35

Euphrates River, 4:58

Eureka Stockade Flag, 1:24

Europe

countries

Albania, 1:10–1:11

Andorra, 1:14–1:15

Austria, 1:46–1:47

Azerbaijan, 1:48–1:49

Belarus, 1:58–1:59

Belgium, 1:60–1:61

Bosnia-Herzegovina, 2:16–2:17

Bulgaria, 2:24–2:25

Croatia, 3:34–3:35

Czech Republic, 3:40–3:41

Denmark, 3:42–3:43

Estonia, 4:10–4:11

Finland, 4:16–4:17

France, 4:18–4:19

Georgia, 4:26–4:27

Germany, 4:28–4:29

Greece, 4:32–4:33

Hungary, 4:48–4:49

Iceland, 4:50–4:51

Ireland, 4:60–4:61

Italy, 5:10–5:11

Kazakhstan, 5:18–5:19

Latvia, 5:34–5:35

Liechtenstein, 5:44–5:45

Lithuania, 5:46–5:47

Luxembourg, 5:48–5:49

Macedonia, 5:50–5:51

Malta, 5:62–5:63

Moldova, 6:18–6:19

Monaco, 6:20–6:21

Netherlands, 6:36–6:37

Norway, 6:56–6:57

Poland, 7:22–7:23

Portugal, 7:24–7:25

Romania, 7:32–7:33

Russia, 7:34–7:35

San Marino, 7:50–7:51

Serbia and Montenegro, 7:58–7:59

Slovakia, 8:14–8:15

Slovenia, 8:16–8:17

Spain, 8:24–8:25

Sweden, 8:34–8:35

Switzerland, 8:36–8:37

Turkey, 8:56–8:57

Ukraine, 9:8–9:9

United Kingdom, 9:12–9:13

Vatican City, 11:60–11:61

dependencies

Azores, 7:26–7:27

Faroe Islands, 3:44–3:45

Gibraltar, 9:34–9:35

Greenland, 3:46

Guernsey, 9:36–9:37

Jersey, 9:38–9:39

Man, Isle of, 9:40–9:41

European Community (EC), 12:14

European Union (EU) flag, 12:14–12:15

Eutaw Flag, 11:34

Evening Star (newspaper), 10:104

Ewe people, 8:48

F

Faisal I, King of Iraq, 4:58

Fakaofo Island (Tokelau), 6:48

Falkland Islands, flag of, 9:32–9:33

Falkland Islands Dependencies, 9:48

Fang (ethnic group), 4:22

Fa Ngum, king of Lao kingdom, 5:32

Faroe Islands, flag of, 3:44–3:45

Fasces, 3:56

Fatima, daughter of Muhammad, 7:54, 12:9, 12:36

Fearn, John, 6:32

Federal Democratic Republic of Ethiopia, **4**:12
Federal Republic of Germany (West Germany), **4**:28
Federated Malay States, **5**:56
Federation of Arab Republics, **3**:58
Federation of Malaya, **5**:56
Federation of Malaysia, **5**:56, **8**:12
Federation of Mali, **7**:56
Federation of South Arabia, **11**:66
Ferdinand V, of Castile, **8**:24, **9**:34, **11**:18
Ferguson, George, **1**:38
Fezzan (Libya), **5**:42
Field, flag of, *See* page 6 of any volume
Fiji, flag of, **4**:14–**4**:15; **8**:60
Finland, flag of, **4**:16–**4**:17
First International Conference of American States, **12**:21
First Montana Infantry regiment, **10**:60
First Troop of Lighthorse, Philadelphia, **11**:29
Fitzgeralds, **4**:60
Flag
  heraldry, *See* page 7 of any volume
  parts of, *See* page 6 of any volume
  raising, *See* page 7 of any volume
  shapes, *See* page 6 of any volume
Flemings, **1**:60
Fleur-de-lis
  France and, **4**:18
  French discovery/settlement flag, **11**:19
  on Quebec flag, **2**:56, **2**:57
  use of symbol, **12**:46–**12**:47
  World Organization of the Scout Movement flag, **12**:26
Florida, flag of, **10**:26–**10**:27
Fluke, Louis Funk, **10**:80
Fly, *See* page 6 of any volume
Folkung family, **8**:34
Fontvieille (Monaco), **6**:20
Fort McHenry flag, **11**:48
Fort Moultrie flag, **11**:33

Fort Moultrie (South Carolina), **10**:88, **11**:33
Fort Sumter (South Carolina), **10**:88
Fowey (British ship), **11**:31
Fraine, John H., **10**:76
France
  Algeria and, **1**:12
  Andorra and, **1**:14
  Arkansas and, **10**:16
  Belgian flag and, **1**:60
  Benin and, **2**:10
  Cambodia and, **2**:30
  Cameroon and, **2**:32
  Central African Republic and, **3**:10
  Chad as colony of, **3**:12
  Comoros and, **3**:24
  Congo (Brazzaville) and, **3**:26
  Côte D'Ivoire and, **3**:32
  discovery/settlement flag of, **11**:19
  Djibouti and, **3**:48
  Dominica and, **3**:50
  European Union flag and, **12**:14
  flag of, **4**:18–**4**:19
  fleurs-de-lis symbol and, **12**:46–**12**:47
  French Polynesia, **4**:20–**4**:21
  Gabon and, **4**:22
  Germany and, **4**:28
  Grenada and, **4**:34
  Guinea and, **4**:38
  Haiti and, **3**:52, **4**:44
  Iowa and, **10**:38
  Kansas and, **10**:40
  Laos and, **5**:32
  Lebanon and, **5**:36
  Libya and, **5**:42
  Louisiana, **10**:44
  Louisiana colony of, **10**:34, **10**:38
  Madagascar as colony of, **5**:52
  Mali and, **5**:60
  Malta and, **5**:62
  Mauritania as colony of, **6**:10
  Missouri and, **10**:58
  Montana and, **10**:60
  Morocco and, **6**:24
  Nebraska bought from, **10**:62

Netherlands and, **6**:36
Niger and, **6**:52
Quebec and, **2**:56
Saint Lucia and, **7**:44
Saint Vincent and the Grenadines and, **7**:46
Senegal and, **7**:56
Seychelles and, **8**:8
Syria and, **8**:38
Togo and, **8**:48
Tunisia and, **8**:54
Vietnam and, **11**:64
France Ancient flag, **12**:46
France Modern flag, **12**:46, **12**:47
Francia, José Gaspar Rodriquez de, **7**:16
Franco, Francisco, **8**:24
Franks, **4**:18
Frederick II, Duke of Austria, **1**:46
Fredonia Rebellion flag, **10**:94
Freemasonry, **7**:20
Fremantle, Charles, **1**:40
French and Indian Wars, **2**:56, **10**:72
French Polynesia, **4**:20–**4**:21
French Revolution of 1789
  events of, **4**:18
  Haiti revolt and, **4**:44
  Italy and, **5**:10
  liberation colors, **12**:34
  Red Banner and, **7**:38
French Somaliland, **3**:48
French Sudan, **5**:60
French Territory of the Afars and Issas, **3**:48
French Tricolor
  French discovery/settlement flag, **11**:19
  French Polynesia's flag, **4**:20
  Gabon's flag and, **4**:22
  Haitian flag and, **4**:44
  information about/illustration of, **4**:18–**4**:19
  and Togo's flag, **8**:48
FRETILIN (Revolutionary Front for an Independent East Timor), **3**:54
Frigate bird, **5**:22, **5**:23
Front de Libération Nationale (Algeria), **1**:12
Front for the Liberation of Mozambique (Frelimo), **6**:26

Fulani (ethnic group), **4**:24, **4**:38, **5**:60
Funchal (Madeira Islands), **7**:28

G
Gabon, flag of, **4**:22–**4**:23
Gadsden, Christopher, **11**:32
Galápagos Islands, **3**:56
Gambia, flag of, **4**:24–**4**:25; **7**:56
Gambia River, **4**:24
Gambier island group, **4**:20
Ganda ethnic group, **8**:62
Gandhi, Mohandas K., **4**:52
Garvey, Marcus, **12**:35
Gauguin, Paul, **4**:20
Gauls, **4**:18
Gautama, Siddhartha, **8**:26
Gauthier, Suzanne, **3**:24
Gebhardt, Dixie C., **10**:38
Gelugspa Buddhism, **6**:22
Geneva Convention, **12**:16
Genghis Khan, **6**:22
Geoctroyeerde West-Indische Compagnie (Dutch West India Company), **11**:21
George II, King of England, **10**:28
George III, King of England, **2**:54
George VI, King of England, **5**:62
George Cross, **5**:62, **5**:63
George Tupou I, King of Tonga, **8**:50
Georgia (country), flag of, **4**:26–**4**:27; **12**:12
Georgia (U.S. state), flag of, **10**:28–**10**:29
Georgian Democratic Republic, **4**:26
German Confederation, **4**:28
German Democratic Republic (East Germany), **4**:28
Germany
  Austria and, **1**:46
  European Union flag and, **12**:14
  flag of, **4**:28–**4**:29
  invasion of Denmark, **3**:44
  Namibia and, **6**:30
  Nauru and, **6**:32
  occupation of Guernsey, **9**:36
  occupation of Jersey, **9**:38
  occupation of Lithuania, **5**:46

occupation of Yugoslavia, 7:58
Palau and, 7:10
Papua New Guinea and, 7:14
Poland and, 7:22
Samoa and, 7:48
Togo and, 8:48
Ghana, flag of, 4:30–4:31, 12:35, 12:54, 12:55
Ghana Empire
control of Mali, 5:60
control of Mauritania, 6:10
Senegal part of, 7:56
Gibraltar, flag of, 9:34–9:35
Gibraltar, Rock of, 9:34
Gibraltar, Strait of, 8:24, 9:34
Gilbert and Ellice Islands Colony, 5:22, 8:60
Gilbert Islands, 5:22
Gill, Harry P., 1:34
Glendower, Owen, 9:20
Glücksborg, House of, 3:42
Gold Coast, 4:30
Golden Arrowhead, 4:42
Goldenrod, 10:42, 10:43
Goshawk, 7:26, 7:27
Grand Army of the Republic, 10:38
Grand Caicos Island (Turks and Caicos Islands), 9:50
Grand Cayman (Cayman Islands), 9:30
Grand Turk Island (Turks and Caicos Islands), 9:50
Grande Comore (Comoros), 3:24
Great Basin (Nevada), 10:64
Great Britain. *See also* United Kingdom
America and, 10:8
Andros Flag, 11:25
Bahrain and, 1:52
Bermuda colony, 9:24
control of Kenya, 5:20
control of Papua New Guinea, 7:14
control of Singapore, 8:12
control of Somalia, 8:20
Dominica and, 3:50
England, 9:14–9:15
Jamaica and, 5:12
Prince Edward Island and, 2:54
rule of India, 4:52

rule of Ireland, 4:60
Saint Lucia and, 7:44
Saint Vincent and the Grenadines and, 7:46
Scotland, 9:18–9:19
Seychelles and, 8:8
South Africa and, 8:22
Swaziland and, 8:32
Syria and, 8:38
United Kingdom's flag, 9:12–9:13
Vermont and, 10:98
Virginia and, 10:100
Wales, 9:20–9:21
Yemen and, 11:66
Great Falls (Montana), 10:60
Great Lakes, 10:52
Great Plains, 10:20, 10:60, 10:70, 10:110
Great Rift Valley, 4:12, 5:54
Great Salt Lake, 10:96
Great Seal of the United States, 10:8
Great Wall of China, 3:16
Great Zimbabwe bird, 11:70, 11:71
Greece
Cyprus and, 3:38
flag of, 4:32–4:33, 12:44, 12:45
Macedonia and, 5:50
Greek Cypriots, 3:38
Greek Orthodox Church, 4:32
Green, Emma Edwards, 10:32
Green Mountain Boys, 10:98, 11:44
Green Mountain Boys flag, 11:28
Green Mountains, 10:98
Greenland, flag of, 3:46–3:47
Grenada, flag of, 4:34–4:35
Grenadines, Saint Vincent and, flag of, 7:46–7:47
Grigorjew, Alexander Wasilijewitsch, 12:12
Grimaldi family, 6:20
Grimaldi, François, 6:20
Grinbergs, Janis, 5:34
Gual, Manuel, 11:62
Guam, flag of, 11:10–11:11
Guaraní Indians, 7:16
Guatemala, flag of, 4:36–4:37
Guayaquil (Ecuador), 3:56
Guernsey, flag of, 9:36–9:37

Guiata Tower (San Marino), 7:50
Guinea, flag of, 4:38–4:39
Guinea-Bissau, 3:8; flag of, 4:40–4:41
Gulf of Aden, 3:48
Gulf of Guinea, 4:30
Gumbs, Jeremiah, 9:22
Guyana, flag of, 4:42–4:43

H
Hadj, Messali, 1:12
Hadley, Paul, 10:36
Haile-Mariam, Mengistu, 4:12
Haile Selassie I, Emperor of Ethiopia, 4:12
Haiti
Dominican Republic and, 3:52
flag of, 4:44–4:45, 12:58, 12:59
Half Moon (ship), 11:21
Han people, 8:40
Hapsburg empire
in Austria, 1:46
control of Hungary, 4:48
rule of Czech Republic, 3:40
Harald Bluetooth, King of Denmark, 3:42
Harold I, King of Norway, 6:56
Harold II, King of England, 9:20
Harris, Charles W., 10:14
Hausa ethnic group, 6:52, 6:54
Hawaii, flag of, 10:30–10:31
Hayden, Charles, 10:14
Hayden, Nancy, 10:14
Helvetians, 8:36
Henry, Patrick, 10:100
Heraldry
College of Arms and, 2:36
Comoros flag design, 3:24
of Czech Republic's flag, 3:40
of Finland's flag, 4:16
of flags, *See* page 7 of any volume
information about, 12:42–12:43
Missouri flag, 10:58
New Brunswick flag design, 2:42
Nunavut flag and, 2:50
Heralds, 12:42
Hercules, Pillars of, 8:24, 9:34

Hershey (Pennsylvania), 10:84
Hicks, Zachary, 1:38
Himalaya, 2:12, 4:52, 6:34
Hindus, 4:52, 4:54
Hindustanis, 8:30
Hispaniola, 3:52, 4:44
Hitler, Adolf, 1:46
Hixon, Francis, 1:28
Hocker, Willie K., 10:16
Hohokam Indians, 10:14
Hoist, *See* page 6 of any volume
Holland, *See* Netherlands
Holy Roman Empire
Germany and, 4:28
Italy part of, 5:10
Slovenia's coat of arms from, 8:16
war flag of, 3:42, 8:36
Honduras, flag of, 4:46–4:47
Hong Kong, flag of, 3:18–3:19
Hopkins, Esek, 11:32
Hopkins flag, 11:32
Hopkinson, Francis, 11:46
Houphouët-Boigny, Félix, 3:32
Huang He (river), 3:16
Hudson, Henry, 10:24, 11:21
Hudson's Bay Company, 10:52
Hungary
Croatia and, 3:34
flag of, 4:48–4:49
rule of Slovakia, 8:14
Husayn ibn 'Ali, King of the Hejaz, 8:38
Hussein, Saddam, 4:58
Hussein, Sharif, 5:16
Hussein Zade, Ali Bey, 1:48
Hutu people, 2:28, 7:40

I
Iberian Peninsula, 7:24, 8:24
Ibingira, Grace, 8:62
Iceland, flag of, 4:50–4:51
Icelanders, 4:50
Idaho, flag of, 10:32–10:33
Idaho Territory, 10:32
Igbo ethnic group, 6:54
Illiniwek Indians, 10:34
Illinois, flag of, 10:34–10:35
Illyrians, 1:10
Imelda, of St. Angela's Convent in Prelate, 2:58
Imperial Russia, flag of, 7:36–7:37
Inca Indians, 3:56, 7:18

India
    conflict with Pakistan, **7**:8
    flag of, **4**:52–4:53
    Nepal and, **6**:34
Indian National Congress, **4**:52
Indian Ocean, **4**:52
Indiana, flag of, **10**:36–10:37
Indiana Territory, **10**:36
Indians. *See also* American
        Indians
    of Alaska, **10**:12
    of Alberta, **2**:36
    of Aruba, **6**:38
    of British Columbia, **2**:38
    of Chile, **3**:14
    of Costa Rica, **3**:30
    of Cuba, **3**:36
    of Dominica, **3**:50
    of Dominican Republic, **3**:52
    of Ecuador, **3**:56
    of El Salvador, **3**:60
    of Fiji, **4**:14
    of Grenada, **4**:34
    of Guatemala, **4**:36
    of Guyana, **4**:42
    of Haiti, **4**:44
    of Honduras, **4**:46
    of Jamaica, **5**:12
    of Manitoba, **2**:40
    of Mauritius, **6**:12
    of Mexico, **6**:14
    of New Brunswick, **2**:42
    of Newfoundland and
        Labrador, **2**:44
    of Northwest Territories,
        2:46
    of Nova Scotia, **2**:48
    of Oman, **6**:58
    of Ontario, **2**:52
    of Panama, **7**:12
    of Paraguay, **7**:16
    of Peru, **7**:18
    of Prince Edward Island,
        2:54
    of Puerto Rico, **11**:14
    of Quebec, **2**:56
    of Saint Kitts and Nevis, **7**:42
    of Saint Lucia, **7**:44
    of Saint Vincent and the
        Grenadines, **7**:46
    of Saskatchewan, **2**:58
    of Trinidad and Tobago, **8**:52
    of Uruguay, **11**:54
    of Venezuela, **11**:62

of Virgin Islands of the
        United States, **11**:16
    of Yukon, **2**:60
Indian Territory, **10**:80
Indonesia
    Association of Southeast
        Asian Nations flag, **12**:10
    control of East Timor, **3**:54
    Dutch control of, **11**:21
    flag of, **4**:54–4:55
Indonesia Association, **4**:54
Indus Valley, **7**:8
Industrial Revolution, **9**:12,
        9:18
Inescutcheon, **9**:16
Ingpen, Robert, **1**:30
Innu, **2**:44
International Alphabet flags,
        12:38–12:39
International Numeral pen-
        nants, **12**:40
International Olympic
        Committee (IOC), **12**:20
International Red Cross and
        Red Crescent flags,
        12:16–12:17
International Union of
        American Republics,
        12:21
Inuit
    of Alaska, **10**:12
    of Newfoundland and
        Labrador, **2**:44
    of Northwest Territories, **2**:46
    of Nunavut, **2**:50
    of Quebec, **2**:56
Inuksuk, **2**:50, **2**:51
IOC (International Olympic
        Committee), **12**:20
Iowa, flag of, **10**:38–10:39
Iqaluit (Nunavut), **2**:50
Iran, flag of, **4**:56–4:57
Iraq, flag of, **4**:58–4:59
Iraqi Governing Council, **4**:58
Ireland
    British Blue Ensign and, **9**:52
    British Red Ensign and, **9**:54
    Commonwealth of Nations
        flag, **12**:13
    flag of, **4**:60–4:61
    Montserrat and, **9**:42–9:43
    Northern Ireland, **9**:16–9:17
    United Kingdom's flag,
        9:12–9:13

Irish Free State, **4**:60, **9**:16
Iroquois Indians, **10**:72
Irrawaddy River, **6**:28
Isabella I, Queen of Spain
    banner of Castile and León,
        11:18
    Gibraltar's coat of arms and,
        9:34
    New Mexico's flag and,
        10:70
    Spain under, **8**:24
Islam
    Algeria and, **1**:12
    Arab League flag, **12**:9
    Azerbaijan and, **1**:48
    in Bangladesh, **1**:54
    in Brunei, **2**:23
    in Comoros, **3**:24
    crescent and star symbols,
        12:48–12:49
    in Egypt, **3**:58
    flag of Maldives and, **5**:58
    in Indonesia, **4**:54
    in Iran, **4**:56
    in Iraq, **4**:58
    Kuwait and, **5**:28
    Libya and, **5**:42
    Mauritania's flag and, **6**:10
    in Oman, **6**:58
    in Pakistan, **7**:8
    pan-Arab colors and,
        12:36
    in Qatar, **7**:30
    in Saudi Arabia, **7**:54
    Somaliland flag and,
        12:31
    in Sudan, **8**:28
    in Tunisia, **8**:54
Isle of Man, **9**:40–9:41
Israel
    flag of, **5**:8–5:9
    Magen David Adom flag,
        12:16
    Palestine and, **12**:30
Issas, **3**:48
Isthmus of Panama, **7**:12
Italy
    control of Somalia, **8**:20
    flag of, **5**:10–5:11
    Libya and, **5**:42
    San Marino, **7**:50
    Vatican City, **11**:60
Ivan Shishman, Czar of
        Bulgaria, **2**:24

J
Jamaica
    Cayman Islands and, **9**:30
    flag of, **5**:12–5:13
    Turks and Caicos Islands
        and, **9**:50
James, Duke of York, **10**:24
James I, King of England, **9**:16
James II, King of England,
        11:25
Jamestown (Virginia), **10**:100
Japan
    attack on Pearl Harbor, **10**:30
    control of Christmas Island,
        1:42
    control of Federated States
        of Micronesia, **6**:16
    control of Marshall Islands,
        6:8
    control of Palau, **7**:10
    control of Taiwan, **8**:40
    flag of, **5**:14–5:15, **12**:50, **12**:51
    Korea and, **5**:26
    Malaysia and, **5**:56
    Myanmar and, **6**:28
    occupation of Philippines,
        7:20
Jasper, William, **11**:33
Jefferson, Thomas, **10**:100
Jersey, flag of, **9**:38–9:39
Jesus Christ
    Banner of Victory and, **9**:14
    flag of Madeira Islands and,
        7:28
    shield of Portugal and, **7**:24
    Tonga's flag and, **8**:50
    Vatican City, **11**:60
Johnson, Willis, **10**:90
Jola (ethnic group), **4**:24
Jonathan, Leabua, **5**:38
Jones, John Paul, **11**:45
Jordan, flag of, **5**:16–5:17
Jordan River Valley (Jordan),
        5:16
Jost van Dyke Island (British
        Virgin Islands), **9**:28
July 4, 1818, U.S. flag, **11**:49
Jutland (Denmark), **3**:42

K
Kabua, Amata, **6**:8
Kabua, Emlain, **6**:8
Kabye people, **8**:48
Kalaallit people, **3**:46

Kalahari Desert, **2**:18, **6**:30
Kalontas, Malon, **11**:58
Kamehameha I, King of Hawaii, **10**:30
Kamehameha III, King of Hawaii, **10**:30
Kanaga emblem, **5**:60
Kansas, **10**:40–**10**:41, **11**:50
KANU (Kenya African National Union), **5**:20
Kariba Dam (Zambia), **11**:68
Karike, Susan, **7**:14
Karyenda (sacred drum), **2**:28
Kashmir region, **7**:8
Kastrioti, Gjegj (Scanderbeg), **1**:10
Kazakhstan, **12**:12; flag of, **5**:18–**5**:19, **12**:52, **12**:53
Keays, Verna, **10**:110
Kentucky, **10**:8; flag of, **10**:42–**10**:43
Kentucky Derby, **10**:42
Kenya African National Union (KANU), **5**:20
Kenya, flag of, **5**:20–**5**:21
Key, Francis Scott, **11**:48
Khmer Empire, **5**:32
Khmer people, **2**:30, **8**:46
Khmer Rouge, **2**:30
Khomeini, Ayatollah Ruhollah, **4**:56
Kievan Rus, **7**:34, **9**:8
Kikuyu people, **5**:20
Kilabuk, Meeka, **2**:50
Kim Il-sung, **5**:24
Kim Jong-il, **5**:24
Kiribati, flag of, **5**:22–**5**:23, **8**:60
Klondike Gold Rush, **2**:60
Knights Hospitallers (religious and military order), **5**:62
Korea, North, flag of, **5**:24–**5**:25, **5**:26
Korea, South, flag of, **5**:24, **5**:26–**5**:27
Korean Peninsula, **5**:24, **5**:26
Korean War, **5**:24, **5**:26
Kublai Khan, **6**:22
Kurds, **4**:58, **8**:56
Kuwait, **4**:58; flag of, **5**:28–**5**:29
Kwajalein Atoll (Marshall Islands), **6**:8
Kyrgyzstan, flag of, **5**:30–**5**:31; **12**:12

L
Labuan island territory (Malaysia), **5**:56
La Condamine (Monaco), **6**:20
La Paz (Bolivia), **2**:14
La Salle, René-Robert Cavelier, Sieur de, **10**:38, **10**:78
La Trinitaria, **3**:52
Ladinos, **4**:36
Lambert, Lynn, **2**:60
Lan Xang, Kingdom of, **5**:32
Lao Lum people, **5**:32
Lao Sung people, **5**:32
Lao Thoeng people, **5**:32
Laos, flag of, **5**:32–**5**:33
Latvia, flag of, **5**:34–**5**:35
Latvian Soviet Socialist Republic, **5**:34
Lawrence, James, **11**:35
League of Nations, **12**:30
Lebanon, flag of, **5**:36–**5**:37, **12**:58
Lee (American cruiser), **11**:31
Leeward Islands
    British Virgin Islands, **9**:28–**9**:29
    coat of arms for, **1**:18
    Montserrat, **9**:42–**9**:43
L'Enfant, Pierre Charles, **10**:104
León (Spain), **8**:24
Leopold II, King of Belgium, **3**:28
Leopold V, Duke of Austria, **1**:46
Lesotho, flag of, **5**:38–**5**:39
Lewis, Edrice, **7**:42
Lewis, Meriwether, **10**:32
Liberation colors, **12**:34
Liberia, flag of, **5**:40–**5**:41
Liberty cap, **4**:44, **7**:16, **10**:72
Libya, flag of, **5**:42–**5**:43
Liechtenstein, flag of, **5**:44–**5**:45
Liechtenstein, Johann-Adam, **5**:44
Light Horse of the City of Philadelphia flag, **11**:29
Line Islands, **5**:22
Lion
    animal symbols on flags, **12**:52, **12**:53
    on banner of Castile and León, **11**:18
    on Bermuda's coat of arms, **9**:24, **9**:25

on Cayman Islands' coat of arms, **9**:30, **9**:31
Conquering Lion of Judah, **4**:12
on Czech Republic's flag, **3**:40
on Fiji's coat of arms, **4**:14
on Finland's flag, **4**:16, **4**:17
on flag of Luxembourg, **5**:48
on Singapore's coat of arms, **8**:12
South Georgia and South Sandwich Islands' flag, **9**:48, **9**:49
Lion and Sun emblem, **4**:56
Lion Flag, **8**:26–**8**:27
Lithuania, **5**:46–**5**:47, **9**:8
Little Cayman (Cayman Islands), **9**:30
Lombards, **8**:16
Lombardy (Italy), **5**:10
Long, James, **10**:94
López, Narciso, **3**:36
Lough Neagh (lake), **9**:16
Louis, King of the Kingdom of Holland, **6**:36
Louis VII, King of France, **12**:46
Louis XIV, King of France, **10**:44
Louis Philippe, King of France, **4**:18
Louisiana, flag of, **10**:44–**10**:45
Louisiana colony, French, **10**:34, **10**:38
Louisiana Purchase
    Arkansas, **10**:16
    Colorado, **10**:20
    Iowa, **10**:38
    North Dakota, **10**:76
    South Dakota, **10**:90
    Wyoming, **10**:110
Lower Peninsula (Michigan), **10**:52
Loyalists, **2**:42
Luang Prabang, Kingdom of, **5**:32
Lützowsche Jäger, **4**:28
Luxembourg, flag of, **5**:48–**5**:49
Luzon Islands (Philippines), **7**:20
Lviv (Ukraine), **9**:8
Lymphad (galley ship), **2**:42, **2**:43

M
Maastricht Treaty, **12**:14
Macao, flag of, **3**:20–**3**:21
Macedones, **5**:50
Macedonia, flag of, **5**:50–**5**:51
Mackinac Bridge, **10**:52
Madagascar, flag of, **5**:52–**5**:53
Madeira Islands, **7**:28–**7**:29
Madrid Protocol, **12**:28
Magellan, Ferdinand, **3**:14
Magen David Adom, **12**:16
Magnolia Flag, **10**:56
Magyars, **4**:48
Mahe (Seychelles), **8**:8
Maine, flag of, **10**:46–**10**:47
Majapahit empire, **4**:54
Majuro (Marshall Islands), **6**:8
Majuro Atoll (Marshall Islands), **6**:8
Malagasy, **5**:52
Malagasy Republic, **5**:52
Malamute dog, **2**:60
Malaspina glacier, **10**:12
Malawi, flag of, **5**:54–**5**:55
Malawi Congress Party, **5**:54
Malay Peninsula, **5**:56, **8**:12
Malay people, **2**:22, **7**:20, **8**:12
Malayan Union, **5**:56
Malaysia, flag of, **5**:56–**5**:57
Maldives, flag of, **5**:58–**5**:59, **12**:48, **12**:49
Mali, flag of, **5**:60–**5**:61
Mali Empire
    control of Mali, **5**:60
    control of Mauritania, **6**:10
    Gambia part of, **4**:24
    Malinke people of, **4**:38
    Senegal part of, **7**:56
Malinke people, **4**:38
Malta, flag of, **5**:62–**5**:63
Man, Isle of, flag of, **9**:40–**9**:41
Manas the Noble, **5**:30
Manchuria, **6**:22
Mandinka (ethnic group), **4**:24
Mangaia Island, **6**:44
Manitoba, flag of, **2**:40–**2**:41
Mao Zedong, **3**:16, **8**:40
Maori, **6**:42
Maple Leaf Flag, **2**:34–**2**:35, **2**:52
Mapuche Indians, **3**:14
Maputo (Mozambique), **6**:26
Margaret, Queen of Denmark, **3**:42

Marinus (Saint Marino), **7**:50
Markoe, Abraham, **11**:29
Marquesas island group, **4**:20
Marshall Islands, flag of,
    6:8–**6**:9; **6**:16
Marxism, **3**:26
Mary, mother of Christ, **8**:50,
    8:56, **12**:48
Maryland, flag of, **10**:48–**10**:49;
    11:47
Mason, Steven T., **10**:52
Massachusetts
    Bedford Flag, **11**:24
    flag of, **10**:50–**10**:51
    Maine as part of, **10**:46
    Taunton Flag, **11**:27
    U.S. flag raised in, **10**:8
    Washington's Cruisers flag,
        11:31
Massachusetts Bay Colony,
    10:50
Mauke Island, **6**:44
Mauritania, flag of, **6**:10–**6**:11;
    12:33
Mauritius, flag of, **6**:12–**6**:13;
    9:26
Maya Empire, **4**:46
Maya Indians, **4**:36, **6**:14
May, Ernest, **10**:90
Mayo Clinic (Rochester,
    Minnesota), **10**:54
Mayotte Island (Comoros), **3**:24
McCarthy, Harry, **11**:39
McKinley, Mount, **10**:12
Mecklenburg (North Carolina),
    10:74
Medina (Saudi Arabia), **7**:54
Mekong River, **5**:32
Melanesians, **4**:14, **7**:14, **8**:18
Meltzer, Frederik, **6**:56
Mendaña, Álvaro de, **8**:60
Mende people, **8**:10
Menelik I, Emperor of Ethiopia,
    4:12
Menelik II, Emperor of
    Ethiopia, **4**:12
Mera, Harry, **10**:70
Mestizos, **6**:14, **6**:50, **7**:12
Mexican-American War, **10**:18
Mexican Empire, **3**:30
Mexico
    Alamo flag and, **11**:36
    Arizona and, **10**:14
    California and, **10**:18

El Salvador and, **3**:60
    flag of, **6**:14–**6**:15
    New Mexico and, **10**:70
    Nicaragua and, **6**:50
    Texas and, **10**:94
Michigan, flag of, **10**:52–**10**:53
Michigan, Lake, **10**:36
Micmac Indians, **2**:54
Micronesia, Federated States of,
    flag of, **6**:16–**6**:17
Micronesians, **5**:22, **6**:8
Middle East
    Afghanistan, **1**:8–**1**:9
    Bahrain, **1**:52–**1**:53
    Cyprus, **3**:38–**3**:39
    Iran, **4**:56–**4**:57
    Iraq, **4**:58–**4**:59
    Israel, **5**:8–**5**:9
    Jordan, **5**:16–**5**:17
    Kuwait, **5**:28–**5**:29
    Kyrgyzstan, **5**:30–**5**:31
    Lebanon, **5**:36–**5**:37
    Saudi Arabia, **7**:54–**7**:55
    Syria, **8**:38–**8**:39
    Turkey, **8**:56–**8**:57
    Turkmenistan, **8**:58–**8**:59
    United Arab Emirates,
        9:10–**9**:11
    Yemen, **11**:66–**11**:67
Milan (Italy), **5**:10
Miller, Mrs. B., **10**:62
Miller, Zel, **10**:28
Mindoro Islands (Philippines),
    7:20
Minneapolis-St. Paul metropol-
    itan area (Minnesota),
    10:54
Minnesota, flag of, **10**:54–**10**:55
Minutemen, **11**:24
Miranda, Francisco de, **11**:62
Miskito Indians, **4**:46
Mississippi, flag of, **10**:56–**10**:57
Mississippi River, **10**:42, **10**:44,
    10:92
Missouri, flag of, **10**:58–**10**:59
Missouri Compromise, **10**:58
Missouri River, **10**:58
Mobutu, president of Congo,
    3:28
Mogollon Indians, **10**:14
Mohéli Island (Comoros), **3**:24
Moldavia, **6**:18, **7**:32
Moldavian Soviet Socialist
    Republic, **6**:18

Moldova, flag of, **6**:18–**6**:19;
    12:12
Monaco, **4**:54; flag of, **6**:20–**6**:21
Monégasques, **6**:20
Mongolia, flag of, **6**:22–**6**:23
Mongols, **6**:22
Mon people, **6**:28, **8**:46
Mont Kartala (Comoros), **3**:24
Montale Tower (San Marino),
    7:50
Montana, flag of, **10**:60–**10**:61
Monte Carlo (Monaco),
    6:20–**6**:21
Montenegro, Serbia and, flag of,
    7:58–**7**:59
Montserrat, flag of, **9**:42–**9**:43
Moon. *See also* Crescent
    on flag of Palau, **7**:10, **7**:11
    on Nepal's flag, **6**:34, **6**:35
    on Uzbekistan's flag,
        11:56–**11**:57
Moors, **6**:10, **8**:26, **9**:34
Moravia (Czech Republic), **3**:40
Mormons (Church of Jesus
    Christ of Latter-day
    Saints), **10**:96
Morocco, flag of, **6**:24–**6**:25;
    12:33
Moseley, William D., **10**:26
Mosquito Coast (Honduras),
    4:46
Moultrie, William, **10**:88,
    11:33
Mound-builder Indians
    of Illinois, **10**:34
    of Indiana, **10**:36
    of Iowa, **10**:38
    of Missouri, **10**:58
    of Ohio, **10**:78
Mount Rushmore National
    Memorial (South
    Dakota), **10**:90
Movement for Democracy
    (Cape Verde), **3**:8
Movement for the Liberation of
    São Tomé and Príncipe
    (MLSTP), **7**:52
Mozambique, flag of, **6**:26–**6**:27,
    12:56
MPLA (Popular Movement for
    the Liberation of Angola),
    1:16
Muhammad Ahmed (Mahdi),
    8:28

Muhammad, Prophet of Islam
    Arab League flag and, **12**:9
    Egypt's flag and, **3**:58
    pan-Arab colors and, **12**:36
    Saudi Arabia's flag and, **7**:54
Mujibur Rahman, **1**:54
Mulattoes, **7**:12
Muscat (Oman), **6**:58
Muslims
    of India, **4**:52
    of Indonesia, **4**:54
    of Iran, **4**:56
    of Iraq, **4**:58
    of Pakistan, **7**:8
    Red Crescent flag, **12**:16,
        12:17
    of Saudi Arabia, **7**:54
    of Sudan, **8**:28
    of Turkey, **8**:56
    of Yemen, **11**:66
Myanmar, flag of, **6**:28–**6**:29
Mynors, William, **1**:42

N
Nacotchtank Indians,
    10:104
Naga people, **8**:26
Namib Desert, **6**:30
Namibia, flag of, **6**:30–**6**:31
Nancy (English ship), **11**:31
Napoleon I, Emperor of France,
    4:28, **9**:46
Narragansett Bay, **10**:86
National Assembly, **9**:20
National Colonial Flag,
    Australia, **1**:24
National Covenant, **5**:36
National Guard, **10**:76
National Opposition Union
    (UNO), **6**:50
National Socialist German
    Workers' (Nazi) Party,
    1:46, **4**:28
Nationalist Party, **3**:16, **8**:40
NATO (North Atlantic Treaty
    Organization) flag,
    12:18–**12**:19
Nauru, flag of, **6**:32–**6**:33
Nazi (National Socialist
    German Workers') Party,
    1:46, **4**:28
Nebraska, flag of, **10**:62–**10**:63
Negritos, **7**:20
Nepal, flag of, **6**:34–**6**:35

Netherlands
  Aruba, **6:**38–**6:**39
  Belgium included in, **1:**60
  control of Suriname, **8:**30
  discovery/settlement flag of,
    11:21
  flag of, **6:**36–**6:**37
  independence from Spain,
    12:34
  Indonesia and, **4:**54
  Luxembourg and, **5:**48
  Netherlands Antilles,
    6:40–**6:**41
  Russian flag and, **7:**34
Netherlands Antilles
  Aruba and, **6:**38
  flag of, **6:**40–**6:**41
Nevada, flag of, **10:**64–**10:**65
Nevis Island, **7:**42, **9:**22
New Brunswick, flag of,
    2:42–**2:**43
New England flag, **11:**26
New France, **11:**19
New Guinea
  Papua New Guinea,
    7:14–**7:**15
  Solomon Islands and, **8:**18
New Hampshire, flag of,
    10:66–**10:**67
New Hebrides, **11:**58
New Jersey, flag of, **10:**68–**10:**69
New Mexico, flag of,
    10:70–**10:**71
New South Wales, flag of,
    1:28–**1:**29
New York City, **10:**72
New York, flag of, **10:**72–**10:**73
New Zealand
  Commonwealth of Nations
    flag, **12:**13
  control of German Samoa,
    7:48
  Cook Islands, **6:**44–**6:**45
  flag of, **6:**42–**6:**43
  Niue, **6:**46–**6:**47
  Tokelau, **6:**48–**6:**49
Newfoundland and Labrador
  Commonwealth of Nations
    flag, **12:**13
  flag of, **2:**44–**2:**45
Newton, Isaac, **9:**14
Niamey (Niger), **6:**52
Nicaragua, flag of, **6:**50–**6:**51
Nicarao, **6:**50

Nicolls, Bruce, **9:**36
Niger, flag of, **6:**52–**6:**53
Nigeria, flag of, **6:**54–**6:**55
Nigerians, **6:**52
Nikoladze, Jakob, **4:**26
Nile River, **3:**58, **8:**28, **8:**62
Niue, flag of, **6:**46–**6:**47
Niyazbekov, Shaken, **5:**18
Nkrumah, Kwame, **4:**30
Nordic Cross. *See* Scandinavian
    Cross
Norfolk Island, flag of, **1:**44–**1:**45
Norfolk pine, **1:**44, **1:**45
Norse, **9:**40
North America
  countries
    Antigua and Barbuda,
      1:18–**1:**19
    Bahamas, **1:**50–**1:**51
    Barbados, **1:**56–**1:**57
    Belize, **2:**8–**2:**9
    Canada, **2:**34–**2:**35
    Costa Rica, **3:**30–**3:**31
    Cuba, **3:**36–**3:**37
    Dominica, **3:**50–**3:**51
    Dominican Republic,
      3:52–**3:**53
    El Salvador, **3:**60–**3:**61
    Grenada, **4:**34–**4:**35
    Guatemala, **4:**36–**4:**37
    Haiti, **4:**44–**4:**45
    Honduras, **4:**46–**4:**47
    Jamaica, **5:**12–**5:**13
    Mexico, **6:**14–**6:**15
    Nicaragua, **6:**50–**6:**51
    Panama, **7:**12–**7:**13
    St. Kitts and Nevis,
      7:42–**7:**43
    St. Lucia, **7:**44–**7:**45
    St. Vincent and the
      Grenadines, **7:**46–**7:**47
    Trinidad and Tobago,
      8:52–**8:**53
    United States, **10:**8–**10:**9
  *territories and dependen-
    cies*
    Anguilla, **9:**22–**9:**23
    Aruba, **6:**38–**6:**39
    Bermuda, **9:**24–**9:**25
    Cayman Islands, **9:**30–**9:**31
    Greenland, **3:**46–**3:**47
    Montserrat, **9:**42–**9:**43
    Netherlands Antilles,
      6:40–**6:**41

Puerto Rico, **11:**14–**11:**15
    Turks and Caicos Islands,
      9:50–**9:**51
    Virgin Islands (U.S.),
      11:16–**11:**17
    Virgin Islands, British,
      9:28–**9:**29
North Atlantic Treaty
    Organization (NATO)
    flag, **12:**18–**12:**19
North Caicos Island (Turks and
    Caicos Islands), **9:**50
North Carolina, flag of,
    10:74–**10:**75
North Dakota, flag of,
    10:76–**10:**77
North Island (New Zealand),
    6:42
North Korea, flag of, **5:**24–**5:**25,
    5:26
North Star, **10:**12–**10:**13, **10:**46
North Vietnam, **11:**64
Northern Ireland
  flag of, **9:**16–**9:**17
  Ireland and, **4:**60
  United Kingdom's flag,
    9:12–**9:**13
Northern Mariana Islands
  Federated States of
    Micronesia and, **6:**16
  flag of, **11:**12–**11:**13
Northern Rhodesia, **11:**68
Northern Territory, flag of,
    1:30–**1:**31
Northern Yemen, **11:**66
Northwest Territories, flag of,
    2:46–**2:**47
Northwest Territory
  Indiana, **10:**36
  Michigan, **10:**52
  Ohio, **10:**78
Norway
  Antarctica and, **12:**28
  control of Faroe Islands, **3:**44
  flag of, **6:**56–**6:**57, **12:**34
  Greenland and, **3:**46
  Iceland and, **4:**50
  Sweden and, **8:**34
Norwegians, **6:**56
Nova Scotia, flag of, **2:**48–**2:**49
Nukunonu Island (Tokelau),
    6:49
Numeral flags, U.S. Navy,
    12:41

Numeral pennants,
    International, **12:**40
Nunavut, flag of, **2:**50–**2:**51
Nyasa, Lake, **5:**54
Nyasaland, **5:**54

O
Oahu (Hawaii), **10:**30
OAS (Organization of American
    States) flag, **12:**21
OAU (Organization of African
    Unity) flag, **12:**8
Oberman, Marvin, **9:**22
Ocean Island, **5:**22
Oglethorpe, James, **10:**28
Ohio, flag of, **10:**78–**10:**79
Ohio River, **10:**42
Okapi, **3:**28
Oklahoma, flag of, **10:**80–**10:**81;
    11:51
Oliver, Marie Elizabeth
    Watkins, **10:**58
Oliver Perry flag, **11:**35
Olive wreath, **8:**58, **8:**59
Olympic flag, **12:**20
Olympic Mountains, **10:**102
Oman, flag of, **6:**58–**6:**59
Omyene (ethnic group), **4:**22
O'Neill family, **9:**16
Ontario, flag of, **2:**52–**2:**53
OPEC (Organization of
    Petroleum Exporting
    Countries) flag, **12:**22
Orange, house of, **6:**36
Order of Christ, **7:**28
Oregon, flag of, **10:**82–**10:**83
Organization of African Unity
    (OAU) flag, **12:**8
Organization of American
    States (OAS) flag, **12:**21
Organization of Petroleum
    Exporting Countries
    (OPEC) flag, **12:**22
Osage Indians, **10:**40–**10:**80
Oscar I, King of Sweden, **6:**56
Ottawa (Ontario), **2:**52
Ottoman Empire
  Albania and, **1:**10
  Algeria and, **1:**12
  Bulgaria and, **2:**24
  crescent and star symbols,
    12:48
  Croatia under control of,
    3:34

Cyprus and, 3:38
Greece and, 4:32
Hungary and, 4:48
Iraq and, 4:58
Jordan part of, 5:16
Lebanon part of, 5:36
Libya and, 5:42
Macedonia part of, 5:50
Moldova and, 6:18
in Qatar, 7:30
Red Crescent flag and, 12:17
Romania and, 7:32
Serbia and Montenegro and, 7:58
Syria and, 8:38
Tunisia and, 8:54
Turkey, 8:56
Yemen and, 11:66
Ovambo people, 6:30
Overseas Territory of South Georgia and South Sandwich Islands, 9:48–9:49
Owen Falls Dam (Uganda), 8:62
Ozark region (Missouri), 10:58

P
Pacific Community flag, 12:23
Pahlavi, Mohammad Reza, 4:56
Pahlavi, Reza Shah, 4:56
PAIGC (African Party for the Independence of Guinea-Bissau and Cape Verde), 3:8, 4:40
Pakistan
Bangladesh as East Pakistan, 1:54
flag of, 7:8–7:9
Palau
Federated States of Micronesia and, 6:16
flag of, 7:10–7:11
Pale, 2:60
Palestine, 5:8, 12:30
Palestinian Arabs, 5:16, 12:30
Palestinian Authority flag, 12:30
Palestinian Liberation Organization (PLO), 12:30
Palmetto, 10:88–10:89
Pan-African colors
of Benin flag, 2:10
of Cape Verde flag, 3:8

of Central African Republic's flag, 3:10
of Chad's flag, 3:12
of Guinea-Bissau's flag, 4:40
of Guinea's flag, 4:38
information about, 12:35
of Mali's flag, 5:60
of Togo's flag, 8:48
Panama Canal, 7:12
Panama, flag of, 7:12–7:13
Pan-American Exposition of 1901, 10:78
Pan American Union, 12:21
Pan-Arab colors
information about, 12:36
of Iraq's flag, 4:58
of Sudan's flag, 8:28
Panmunjom (Korean peninsula), 5:24
Pan-Slavic colors
described, 12:37
Serbia and Montenegro and, 7:58
of Slovakia's flag, 8:14
of Slovenia's flag, 8:16
Papal States, 11:60
Papua New Guinea, flag of, 7:14–7:15
Paraguay, flag of, 7:16–7:17
Paris Commune, 7:38
Paris (France), 4:18
Partisans, 7:58
Pathet Lao, 5:32
Patriarchal cross, 8:14
Peacock, 6:28
Pearl Harbor (Hawaii), 5:14, 10:30
Pearson, Lester B., 2:34
Pedro I, King of Brazil, 2:20
Pelican, 10:44–10:45
Peninsular Malaysia, 5:56
Pennant, 4:42
Pennine Mountains, 9:14
Pennsylvania
Delaware and, 10:24
flag of, 10:84–10:85
People's African League for Independence, 3:48
People's Front for Democracy and Justice, 4:8
People's Republic of China
establishment of, 8:40
flag of, 3:16–3:17

People's Republic of Kampuchea, 2:30
People's Revolutionary Party, Benin, 2:10
People's United Party, 2:8
Perry, Oliver Hazard, 11:35
Persian Empire, 4:56
Persian Gulf War of 1991, 4:58
Persians, 8:42
Peru, flag of, 7:18–7:19
Peter the Great, Czar of Russia
flag of Russia, 7:34, 7:36, 12:37
Serbia and Montenegro flag and, 7:58
Philadelphia, Light Horse of the City of, flag of, 11:29
Philip I, King of France, 12:46
Philip II, King of Macedon, 5:50
Philippines
Association of Southeast Asian Nations flag, 12:10
flag of, 7:20–7:21
Phoenicians, 5:36, 8:54
Phoenix Islands, 5:22
Phosphates, 6:32
Pichette, Robert, 2:42
Piedmont region (Georgia), 10:28
Piedmont region (Maryland), 10:48
Piedmont region (New Jersey), 10:68
Pilgrims, 10:50, 11:20
Pillars of Hercules, 8:24, 9:34
Pine, Benjamin, 1:18
Pine tree
on flag of New England, 11:26
on Maine's flag, 10:46, 10:47
on Massachusetts' flag, 10:50
on Washington's Cruisers flag, 11:31
Pinto da Costa, Manuel, 7:52
Pitcairn Island, 9:44
Pitcairn Islands Group, flag of, 9:44–9:45
Pitcairn, Robert, 9:44
Pitons (volcanoes of Saint Lucia), 7:44
Plains Indians, 10:38
Plantagenet, House of, 9:39
Plant symbols, 12:58–12:59

PLO (Palestinian Liberation Organization), 12:30
Poland
flag of, 7:22–7:23
Lithuania and, 5:46
rule of Ukraine, 9:8
Polders, 6:36
Poles, 7:22
Polisario Front, 12:33
Polynesians
of American Samoa, 11:8
of Cook Islands, 6:44
of Hawaii, 10:30
of New Zealand, 6:42
of Niue, 6:46
of Pitcairn Island, 9:44
of Samoa, 7:48
of Tonga, 8:50
of Tuvalu, 8:60
Pomare IV, Queen of Tahiti, 4:20
Ponce de León, Juan, 11:18
Pope, 11:60
Popular Movement for the Liberation of Angola (MPLA), 1:16
Porto Santo (Madeira Islands), 7:28
Portugal
Angola and, 1:16
Azores, 7:26–7:27
Brazil and, 2:20
Cameroon and, 2:32
Cape Verde and, 3:8
East Timor and, 3:54
Equatorial Guinea and, 3:62
flag of, 7:24–7:25
Guinea-Bissau and, 4:40
Macao and, 3:20
Madeira Islands, 7:28–7:29
Mozambique and, 6:26
Oman and, 6:58
Portuguese explorers in Ghana, 4:30
São Tomé and Príncipe and, 7:52
Seychelles and, 8:8
Uruguay and, 11:54
Portuguese
control of Kenya, 5:20
discovery of Saint Helena, 9:46
in Sierra Leone, 8:10
Praia (Cape Verde), 3:8

Pratt, Christopher, **2**:44
Prescod, Grantley, **1**:56
Prince Edward Island, flag of, **2**:54–**2**:55
Príncipe, São Tomé and, **7**:52–**7**:53
Protestants, **9**:16
Providenciales Island (Turks and Caicos Islands), **9**:50
Prussia, **7**:22
Puerto Ricans, **10**:72
Puerto Rico, flag of, **11**:14–**11**:15
Puritans, **10**:50, **10**:86
Pygmies, **3**:62

Q
Qadhafi, Muammar Muhammad al-, **5**:42
Qatar, flag of, **7**:30–**7**:31
Qing (Manchu) dynasty, **3**:16
Quebec, flag of, **2**:56–**2**:57
Queensland, flag of, **1**:32–**1**:33
Quetzal (Guatemalan bird), **4**:36
Qur'ān, **5**:16, **5**:42, **6**:24

R
Raleigh (frigate), **10**:66
Rama VI, King of Thailand, **8**:46
Rampant lion
    on Czech Republic's flag, **3**:40
    on Finland's coat of arms, **4**:16
    on flag of Luxembourg, **5**:48
    on South Georgia and South Sandwich Islands' flag, **9**:48
Rarotonga Island, **6**:44
Ras al Khaymah (United Arab Emirates), **9**:10–**9**:11
Rastafarianism, **5**:12
Red Banner
    Russia and, **7**:34
    Russian Revolution and, **7**:38
    Tajikistan's flag, **8**:42
    Turkmenistan's flag, **8**:58
    Ukraine's flag, **9**:8
Red Crescent flag, **12**:16, **12**:17
Red Cross flag, **12**:16–**12**:17
Redonda island, **1**:18
Red River Valley (North Dakota), **10**:76

Red Sea, **3**:48
Reeves, LeRoy, **10**:92
Religion. *See* specific religions
Republic of China, **3**:16
Republic of Cyprus, **3**:38
Republic of Ireland, **4**:60, **9**:16
Republic of the Congo (Brazzaville), **3**:26
Republic of the Congo (Kinshasa), **3**:28
Revolutionary Front for an Independent East Timor (FRETILIN), **3**:54
Revolutionary War in America. *See also* United States, colonial and Revolutionary War flags
    Connecticut and, **10**:22
    Continental Colors flag, **11**:45
    Delaware in, **10**:24
    heraldry symbols and, **10**:48
    liberation colors, **12**:34
    Maryland and, **10**:48
    Massachusetts and, **10**:50
    New Brunswick and, **2**:42
    New Jersey's flag and, **10**:68
    New York in, **10**:72
    North Carolina in, **10**:74
    Pennsylvania in, **10**:84
    Rhode Island and, **10**:86
    South Carolina and, **10**:88
    Third Maryland Regiment flag, **11**:47
    U.S. flag and, **10**:8
    Vermont and, **10**:98
    Virginia in, **10**:100
Reykjavik (Iceland), **4**:50
Rhode Island, flag of, **10**:86–**10**:87
Rhode Island regiment flag, **11**:30
Rhodes, Cecil, **11**:68
Richmond (Virginia), **10**:100
Río Muni (Equatorial Guinea), **3**:62
Roanoke Island (North Carolina), **10**:74
Robarts, John, **2**:52
Robinson, Doane, **10**:90
Rocky Mountains, **10**:32, **10**:60, **10**:70, **10**:96, **10**:102, **10**:110
Roger I, Count of Sicily, **5**:62

Roman Catholic Church
    in Ireland, **4**:60, **9**:16
    in Italy, **5**:10
    Paraguay and, **7**:16
    Vatican City, **11**:60
Roman Empire, **5**:10, **7**:32
Romania
    control of Moldova, **6**:18
    flag of, **7**:32–**7**:33
Romans, **4**:18, **9**:18
Rome, **9**:20
Rome (Italy), **11**:60
Royal Greenland Trading Company, **3**:46
Royal Navy, **9**:52, **9**:54
Rushmore National Memorial, Mount (South Dakota), **10**:90
Russia
    Armenia and, **1**:22
    Azerbaijan and, **1**:48
    Belarus and, **1**:58
    Bulgarian flag and, **2**:24
    Commonwealth of Independent States flag, **12**:12
    control of Finland, **4**:16
    control of Georgia, **4**:26
    control of Turkmenistan, **8**:58
    Estonia and, **4**:10
    flag of, **7**:34–**7**:35, **12**:37
    flag of imperial Russia, **7**:36–**7**:37
    Kyrgyzstan and, **5**:30
    Latvia and, **5**:34
    Lithuania and, **5**:46
    rule of Poland, **7**:22
    rule of Tajikistan, **8**:42
    rule of Ukraine, **9**:8
    Union of Soviet Socialist Republics, **7**:38
Russian-American Company flag, **11**:23
Russian Revolution, **4**:10, **4**:16, **7**:38
Russian Socialist Federated Soviet Republic, **7**:38
Rwanda, flag of, **7**:40–**7**:41

S
Sab clans, **8**:20
Saba Island, **6**:40
Sabah (Malaysia), **5**:56

Sacre Coeur (Sacred Heart of Jesus), **2**:56
Sadat, Anwar el-, **5**:42
SADR (Saharawi Arab Democratic Republic), **12**:33
Safi al-Din al-Hilli, **5**:28, **12**:36
Sahara desert
    in Algeria, **1**:12
    in Libya, **5**:42
    in Mali, **5**:60
    in Mauritania, **6**:10
    in Niger, **6**:52
Saharawi Arab Democratic Republic (SADR), **12**:33
Sahel (Mali), **5**:60
Said, Ahmad bin, **6**:58
Said, Al Bu, family of, **6**:58
Said, Qaboos bin, **6**:58
St. Andrew. *See* Cross of St. Andrew
St. Augustine (Florida), **10**:26
St. Christopher Island. *See* St. Kitts and Nevis
St. Croix (Virgin Islands of the United States), **11**:16
St. Eustatius Island, **6**:40
St. George. *See* Cross of St. George
St. John (Virgin Islands of the United States), **11**:16
St. Martin Island, **6**:40
St. Omer, Dunstan, **7**:44
St. Patrick. *See* Cross of St. Patrick
St. Peter's Basilica, **11**:60
St. Stephen's Crown, **4**:48
St. Thomas (Virgin Islands of the United States), **11**:16
St. Vincent Island, **7**:46
Saint Domingue. *See* Haiti
Saint Helena, flag of, **9**:46–**9**:47
Saint Kitts and Nevis, flag of, **7**:42–**7**:43
Saint Kitts Island, **7**:42–**7**:43, **9**:22
Saint Lucia, flag of, **7**:44–**7**:45
Saint Ursula, **9**:28
Saint Vincent and the Grenadines, flag of, **7**:46–**7**:47
Sakalavas (rulers of Madagascar), **5**:52

Saladin (ruler of Egypt and Syria), 3:58
Salt Cay Island (Turks and Caicos Islands), 9:50
Salt Lake City (Utah), 10:96
Saltire
    on Alabama's flag, 10:10, 10:11
    on Burundi's flag, 2:28
    on Florida's flag, 10:26, 10:27
    on Irish flag, 4:60
    on Jamaica's flag, 5:12
    on Jersey's flag, 9:38, 9:39
    on Scotland's flag, 9:18–9:19
Samaal clans, 8:20
Sami people, 4:16, 6:56, 8:34
Samoa
    flag of, 7:48–7:49
    Niue and, 6:46
    Tuvalu and, 8:60
Samoa, American
    flag of, 11:8–11:9
    islands of, 7:48
Samoans, 5:22
Samuel, Reginald, 1:18
San people, 6:30
San Marino
    flag of, 7:50–7:51
    location, 5:10
San Martín, José de, 3:14, 3:56, 7:18
Sandinista movement, flag of, 6:50
Sankara, Thomas, 2:26
Santiago (Chile), 3:14
Santo Domingo (Dominican Republic), 3:52
Sanusi brotherhood, 5:42
São Tiago Island (Cape Verde), 3:8
São Tomé and Príncipe, flag of, 7:52–7:53
Sarawak (Malaysia), 5:56
Sardinia, 5:10
Sarmatians, 6:18
Saskatchewan, 2:58–2:59
Saud, Abd al-Azin bin, 7:54
Saud dynasty, 7:54
Saudi Arabia, flag of, 7:54–7:55
Savai'i Island (Samoa), 7:48
Savannah (Georgia), 10:28
Scanderbeg (Gjergj Kastrioti), 1:10

Scandinavian Cross
    on Denmark's flag, 3:42
    on Faroe Islands flag, 3:44
    on Finland's flag, 4:16
    on Iceland's flag, 4:50
    on Sweden's flag, 8:34
    use of, 12:44
Scandinavians, 6:56
Schywz, canton of, 8:36
Scotland
    British Blue Ensign and, 9:52
    British Red Ensign and, 9:54
    flag of, 9:18–9:19
    Nova Scotia and, 2:48
    United Kingdom's flag, 9:12–9:13
Scythians, 6:18
Seal. *See also* State seal
    of British Columbia, 2:38
    of Jamaica, 5:12
    of Prince Edward Island, 2:54
    treasury seal of Paraguay, 7:16
Seal of Solomon, 6:24
Sea Venture (British ship), 9:24
Semites, 8:38
Senegal
    flag of, 7:56–7:57
    part of Federation of Mali, 5:60
Serahuli (ethnic group), 4:24
Serajul Alam, 1:54
Serbia and Montenegro, flag of, 7:58–7:59
Serbs, 2:16
Serbs, Croats, and Slovenes, Kingdom of, 7:58, 8:16
Settlement flags. *See* Discovery and settlement flags
1777, Stars and Stripes, flag of, 11:46
Seychelles, flag of, 8:8–8:9
Seychelles People's Progressive Front (SPPF), 8:8
Seychelles People's United Party (SPUP), 8:8
Shackleton, Ernest, 9:48
Shahada, 5:28, 7:54
Shakespeare, William, 9:14
Shamrock, 9:42
Shannon (battleship), 11:35
Shapes, flag, *See* page 6 of any volume

Sheba, Queen of, 4:12
Shellback, Louis, 10:64
Shevardnadze, Eduard, 4:26
Shield of arms, 9:42, 9:43
Shogun (ruler), 5:14
Siam, 8:46
Sicily, 5:10
Sidney, Algernon, 10:50
Siegfried, count of Ardennes, 5:48
Sierra Leone, flag of, 8:10–8:11
Sierra Leone Peninsula, 8:10
Sierra Nevada mountains, 10:18
Silk Road, 11:56
Simitière, Eugène du, 10:68
Sinai Peninsula (Egypt), 3:58
Singapore, flag of, 8:12–8:13; 12:10
Sinhalese people
    flag of, 12:52, 12:53
    of Maldives, 5:58
    of Sri Lanka, 8:26
Sioux Indians, 10:54, 10:76
Sisserous, 3:50, 3:51
Slavery
    in Alabama, 10:10
    in Arkansas, 10:16
    Cape Verde and, 3:8
    Central African Republic and, 3:10
    in Congo, 3:28
    Dominica and, 3:50
    Dominican Republic/Haiti and, 3:52
    in Florida, 10:26
    freed slaves in Liberia, 5:40
    in Georgia (U.S. state), 10:28
    in Guyana, 4:42
    in Haiti, 4:44
    Kansas and, 10:40
    in Mauritius, 6:12
    in Mississippi, 10:56
    in Saint Kitts and Nevis, 7:42
    in Saint Vincent and the Grenadines, 7:46
    São Tomé and Príncipe and, 7:52
    Sierra Leone and, 8:10
    slaves from Gambia, 4:24
    slave trade in Nigeria, 6:54
    in Trinidad and Tobago, 8:52
    in United States, 10:8
    West Virginia and, 10:106
Slavs, 7:34, 7:58

Slovakia
    Czech Republic and, 3:40
    flag of, 8:14–8:15
Slovenia, flag of, 8:16–8:17
Smith, John, 10:104
Smith, Whitney, 4:42, 12:28
Sobhuza II, King of Swaziland, 8:32
Socialism, 3:24, 4:12
Solomon Islands, flag of, 8:18–8:19
Solomon, King of Israel, 4:12
Somalia, flag of, 8:20–8:21
Somaliland, flag of, 12:31
Songhai Empire
    control of Mali, 5:60
    control of Mauritania, 6:10
    in Niger, 6:52
    Senegal part of, 7:56
Soto, Hernando de, 11:18
South Africa
    Botswana and, 2:18
    Commonwealth of Nations flag, 12:13
    flag of, 8:22–8:23
    Namibia and, 6:30
South America
    countries
    Argentina, 1:20–1:21, 12:50, 12:51
    Bolivia, 2:14–2:15
    Brazil, 2:20–2:21
    Chile, 3:14–3:15
    Colombia, 3:22–3:23
    Ecuador, 3:56–3:57
    Guyana, 4:42–4:43
    Paraguay, 7:16–7:17
    Peru, 7:18–7:19
    Suriname, 8:30–8:31
    Uruguay, 11:54–11:55
    Venezuela, 11:62–11:63
    dependency or territory
    Falkland Islands, 9:32–9:33
Southampton Island, 2:50
South Australia, flag of, 1:34–1:35
South Caicos Island (Turks and Caicos Islands), 9:50
South Carolina
    Eutaw Flag, 11:34
    flag of, 10:88–10:89
    Fort Moultrie flag, 11:33
South Dakota, flag of, 10:90–10:91

South Georgia and South Sandwich Islands, flag of, **9**:48–**9**:49

South Island (New Zealand), **6**:42

South Korea, **5**:24; flag of, **5**:26–**5**:27

South Pacific Commission, **12**:23

South Sandwich Islands, South Georgia and, **9**:48–**9**:49

South Vietnam, **11**:64

South West Africa People's Organization (SWAPO), **6**:30

Southeast Asia
    Association of Southeast Asian Nations flag, **12**:10
    Brunei, **2**:22–**2**:23
    Cambodia, **2**:30–**2**:31
    East Timor, **3**:54–**3**:55
    Indonesia, **4**:54–**4**:55
    Laos, **5**:32–**5**:33
    Malaysia, **5**:56–**5**:57
    Myanmar, **6**:28–**6**:29
    Philippines, **7**:20–**7**:21
    Singapore, **8**:12–**8**:13
    Thailand, **8**:46–**8**:47
    Vietnam, **11**:64–**11**:65

Southern Cross
    on Australian Capital Territory's flag, **1**:26, **1**:27
    on Australia's flag, **1**:24
    on Christmas Island flag, **1**:42, **1**:43
    on flag of Niue, **6**:46
    on flag of Papua New Guinea, **7**:14–**7**:15
    on flag of Samoa, **7**:48–**7**:49
    on New Zealand's flag, **6**:42
    on Northern Territory flag, **1**:30, **1**:31
    use of star symbol, **12**:54
    on Victoria's flag, **1**:38

Southern Rhodesia, **11**:70

Southern Yemen, **11**:66

Soviet Union
    Angola and, **1**:16
    Armenia and, **1**:22
    Azerbaijan and, **1**:48
    Commonwealth of Independent States flag, **12**:12
    Estonia and, **4**:10

flag of, **7**:38–**7**:39

Georgia part of, **4**:26

Kazakhstan and, **5**:18

Kyrgyzstan and, **5**:30

Latvia and, **5**:34

Lithuania and, **5**:46

Moldova and, **6**:18

Mongolia and, **6**:22

NATO and, **12**:18

North Korea and, **5**:24

Poland and, **7**:22

Red Cross/Red Crescent flag in, **12**:17

Russia in, **7**:34

Tajikistan and, **8**:42

Turkmenistan and, **8**:58

Ukraine and, **9**:8

Uzbekistan, **11**:56

Soyonbo (Mongolian emblem), **6**:22

Spain
    Andorra and, **1**:14
    Argentina and, **1**:20
    Arkansas and, **10**:16
    Bolivia and, **2**:14
    British Virgin Islands and, **9**:28
    California and, **10**:18
    Chile and, **3**:14
    Colombia and, **3**:22
    Costa Rica and, **3**:30
    Cuba and, **3**:36
    discovery/settlement flag of, **11**:18
    Dominican Republic and, **3**:52
    Ecuador and, **3**:56
    El Salvador and, **3**:60
    Equatorial Guinea and, **3**:62
    flag of, **8**:24–**8**:25
    Florida, Spanish in, **10**:26
    Gibraltar and, **9**:34
    Guam and, **11**:10
    Guatemala and, **4**:36
    Haiti and, **4**:44
    Honduras and, **4**:46
    Jamaica and, **5**:12
    Mexico and, **6**:14
    Montserrat and, **9**:42
    Morocco and, **6**:24
    Netherlands and, **6**:36, **12**:34
    New Mexico and, **10**:70
    Nicaragua and, **6**:50
    Palau and, **7**:10

Panama and, **7**:12

Paraguay and, **7**:16

Peru and, **7**:18

Philippines and, **7**:20

Portugal and, **7**:24

Puerto Rico and, **11**:14

Texas and, **10**:94

Trinidad and Tobago and, **8**:52

Uruguay and, **11**:54

Venezuela and, **11**:62

Spanish-American War
    Cuba and, **3**:36
    First Montana Infantry regiment, **10**:60
    Guam and, **11**:10
    Philippines and, **7**:20
    Puerto Rico and, **11**:14

Spanish Cross of Burgundy, **4**:60

Sparks, John, **10**:64

Spence, Joseph, **10**:100

SPPF (Seychelles People's Progressive Front), **8**:8

SPUP (Seychelles People's United Party), **8**:8

Sri Lanka, flag of, **8**:26–**8**:27, **12**:52, **12**:53

Stainless Banner, **11**:40, **11**:42

Stark, John, **11**:44

Star of David, **5**:8–**5**:9

Star of Verghina, **5**:50

Stars
    on Alaska's flag, **10**:12–**10**:13
    on Arizona's flag, **10**:14–**10**:15
    on Arkansas' flag, **10**:16–**10**:17
    on Aruba's flag, **6**:38–**6**:39
    on Bennington Flag, **11**:44
    on Cook Islands' flag, **6**:44–**6**:45
    crescent and star symbols, **12**:48–**12**:49
    on European Union's flag, **12**:14–**12**:15
    on Georgia's flag, **10**:28–**10**:29
    on Indiana's flag, **10**:36–**10**:37
    on Missouri's flag, **10**:58–**10**:59
    on Nauru's flag, **6**:32–**6**:33

on Nevada's flag, **10**:64–**10**:65

on Netherlands Antilles' flag, **6**:40–**6**:41

on Niue's flag, **6**:46–**6**:47

on Northern Mariana Islands' flag, **11**:12–**11**:13

on Ohio's flag, **10**:78–**10**:79

on Oregon's flag, **10**:82–**10**:83

on Pakistan's flag, **7**:8–**7**:9

on Panama's flag, **7**:12–**7**:13

on Philippines' flag, **7**:20–**7**:21

on Rhode Island's flag, **10**:86–**10**:87

on Singapore's flag, **8**:12–**8**:13

on Solomon Islands' flag, **8**:18–**8**:19

on Somalia's flag, **8**:20–**8**:21

on Suriname's flag, **8**:30–**8**:31

on Syria's flag, **8**:38–**8**:39

on Tajikistan's flag, **8**:42–**8**:43

on Tennessee's flag, **10**:92–**10**:93

on Texas' flag, **10**:94–**10**:95

on Togo's flag, **8**:48–**8**:49

on Tokelau's flag, **6**:48–**6**:49

on Tunisia's flag, **8**:54–**8**:55

on Turkey's flag, **8**:56–**8**:57

on Turkmenistan's flag, **8**:58–**8**:59

use of symbol, **12**:54–**12**:55

on U.S. flag, **10**:8–**10**:9

on USSR's flag, **7**:38–**7**:39

on Venezuela's flag, **11**:62–**11**:63

on Vietnam's flag, **11**:64–**11**:65

on Washington, D.C.'s flag, **10**:104–**10**:105

on Zimbabwe's flag, **11**:70–**11**:71

Stars and Bars flag, Confederate Georgia's flag and, **10**:28
    information about, **11**:40
    North Carolina's flag and, **10**:74

Stars and Stripes Flag
    of 1777, **11**:46
    1859 to 1861 flag, **11**:50

1908 to 1912 flag, **11**:51
1912 to 1959 flag, **11**:52
1959 to 1960 flag, **11**:53
1960 to present, **10**:9
Continental Colors, **11**:45
description of/illustration of, **10**:8–**10**:9
Fort McHenry flag, **11**:48
July 4, 1818 flag, **11**:49
Third Maryland Regiment, **11**:47
State flags. *See* United States
State of Greater Lebanon, **5**:36
State seal
  of Florida, **10**:26–**10**:27
  of Georgia, **10**:28–**10**:29
  of Idaho, **10**:32–**10**:33
  of Illinois, **10**:34–**10**:35
  of Kansas, **10**:40–**10**:41
  of Kentucky, **10**:42–**10**:43
  of Minnesota, **10**:54–**10**:55
  of Missouri, **10**:58
  of Montana, **10**:60–**10**:61
  of Nebraska, **10**:62–**10**:63
  of New Hampshire, **10**:66–**10**:67
  of Oregon, **10**:82–**10**:83
  of South Dakota, **10**:90–**10**:91
  of Utah, **10**:96–**10**:97
  of Vermont, **10**:98
  of Virginia, **10**:100–**10**:101
  of Washington, **10**:102–**10**:103
  of West Virginia, **10**:106
  of Wyoming, **10**:110–**10**:111
State shield, of Alabama, **10**:10
Straits Settlements, **1**:42, **8**:12
Strong, John, **9**:32
Sucre (Bolivia), **2**:14
Sudan, flag of, **8**:28–**8**:29
Suez Canal, **3**:58
Sukhothai Kingdom, **8**:46
Sun
  on Japan's flag, **5**:14–**5**:15
  on Kazakhstan's flag, **5**:18–**5**:19
  on Kiribati's flag, **5**:22–**5**:23
  on Kyrgyzstan's flag, **5**:30–**5**:31
  on Macedonia's flag, **5**:50
  on Malawi's flag, **5**:54–**5**:55
  of Namibia's flag, **6**:30–**6**:31
  on Nepal's flag, **6**:34–**6**:35

  on New Mexico's flag, **10**:70–**10**:71
  on Niger's flag, **6**:52
  on Philippines' flag, **7**:20–**7**:21
  on Rwanda's flag, **7**:40–**7**:41
  on Uruguay's flag, **11**:54–**11**:55
  use of symbol, **12**:50–**12**:51
Sun Yat-sen, **8**:40
Sunflower, **10**:40–**10**:41
Suriname, flag of, **8**:30–**8**:31
Susu (ethnic group), **4**:38
Swan, **1**:40–**1**:41
Swan, Conrad, **2**:54
SWAPO (South West Africa People's Organization), **6**:30
Swastika flag, **4**:28
Swazi people, **8**:32
Swazi Pioneer Corps, **8**:32
Swaziland, flag of, **8**:32–**8**:33
Sweden
  control of Finland, **4**:16
  discovery/settlement flag of, **11**:22
  flag of, **8**:34–**8**:35
  rule of Norway, **6**:56
Swiss Alps, **8**:36
Swiss Confederation, **8**:36
Switzerland
  flag of, **8**:36–**8**:37
  International Red Cross flag and, **12**:16
Symbols
  animals, **12**:52–**12**:53
  crescent and star, **12**:48–**12**:49
  cross, **12**:44–**12**:45
  fleurs-de-lis, **12**:46–**12**:47
  plants, **12**:58–**12**:59
  stars, **12**:54–**12**:55
  sun, **12**:50–**12**:51
  tools, **12**:56–**12**:57
Syria
  flag of, **8**:38–**8**:39
  United Arab Republic and, **3**:58
Syrian Desert, **5**:16

T
Taconic Mountains, **10**:50
T'aeguk (Korean symbol), **5**:26
Tahiti (French Polynesia), **4**:20

Taipa Island, **3**:20
Taiwan, flag of, **8**:40–**8**:41
Tajikistan, flag of, **8**:42–**8**:43; **12**:12
Talcott, Charles and Grant, **10**:102
Taliban, **1**:8
Tamasese, King of Samoa, **7**:48
Tamil people, **8**:26
Tanganyika, **8**:44
Tanganyika African National Union, **8**:44
Tanzania, flag of, **8**:44–**8**:45
Tasman, Abel, **1**:36
Tasmania, flag of, **1**:36–**1**:37
Taufa'ahau, King of Tonga, **8**:50
Taunton Flag, **11**:27
Taunton (Massachusetts), **11**:27
Teff (grain), **4**:8
Temne people, **8**:10
Tennessee, flag of, **10**:92–**10**:93
Tenochtitlán (Mexico), **6**:14
Territorial Council, Northwest Territories, **2**:46
Texas
  Alamo flag, **11**:36
  flag of, **10**:94–**10**:95
  Texas Navy flag, **11**:37
Texas Navy flag, **11**:37
Thailand
  Association of Southeast Asian Nations flag, **12**:10
  flag of, **8**:46–**8**:47
Theocracy, **8**:28
Third Maryland Regiment flag, **11**:47
Thoburn, Joseph, **10**:80
Thomson, Charles, **10**:8
Three Kingdoms, **5**:26
Tiara, **11**:60
Tibetans, **2**:12, **6**:34
Tigris river, **4**:58
Titano, Mount, **7**:50
Tito, Josip Broz, **7**:58
Tobago, **8**:52
Togo, flag of, **8**:48–**8**:49
Tokelau, flag of, **6**:48–**6**:49
Toltec Indians, **6**:14
Tomas, Stjepan, King of Bosnia, **2**:16
Tonga
  flag of, **8**:50–**8**:51, **12**:44, **12**:45
  Niue and, **6**:46

Tool symbols, **12**:56–**12**:57
Topelius, Zachris, **4**:16
Torch, **10**:36, **10**:37
Tortola Island (British Virgin Islands), **9**:28
Toucouleur ethnic group, **5**:60, **6**:10
Touré, Sékou, **4**:38
Transjordan Plateau (Jordan), **5**:16
Treaty of Utrecht, **9**:34
Triglav, Mount, **8**:16
Trinidad and Tobago, flag of, **8**:52–**8**:53
Tripolitania (Libya), **5**:42
Triskelion, **9**:40, **9**:41
Tristan da Cunha group, **9**:46
TRNC (Turkish Republic of Northern Cyprus), **3**:38, **12**:32
Trucial States, **9**:10
Trust Territory of the Pacific Islands (TTPI)
  Federated States of Micronesia, **6**:16
  Marshall Islands, **6**:8
  Northern Mariana Islands, **11**:12
  Palau, **7**:10
Tsunamis, **3**:14
TTPI. *See* Trust Territory of the Pacific Islands
Tuamotu island group, **4**:20
Tuareg Empire, **6**:52
Tu'i Tonga, **8**:50
Tunis (Tunisia), **8**:54
Tunisia, flag of, **8**:54–**8**:55
Turkey
  control of Hungary, **4**:48
  Cyprus and, **3**:38
  flag of, **8**:56–**8**:57, **12**:48
Turkish Cypriots, **3**:38
Turkish Republic of Northern Cyprus (TRNC), **3**:38; flag of, **12**:32
Turkmen Soviet Socialist Republic, **8**:58
Turkmenistan, flag of, **8**:58–**8**:59; **12**:12
Turks, **8**:56. *See also* Ottoman Empire
Turks and Caicos Islands, flag of, **9**:50–**9**:51
Tutsi people, **2**:28, **7**:40

Tutuila Island (American Samoa), **11**:8

Tuvalu, **5**:22; flag of; **8**:60–**8**:61

Tvrtko I, King of Bosnia, **2**:16

Twa people, **7**:40

Twitchell, Ralph E., **10**:70

Tynwald Court, **9**:40

U

UAE (United Arab Emirates), flag of, **9**:10–**9**:11

UAR (United Arab Republic) flag of, **3**:58

Syria in, **8**:38

Ubangi-Shari (French colony, now Central African Republic), **3**:10

Uganda, flag of, **8**:62–**8**:63

Uganda People's Congress (UPC), **8**:62

Ukraine

Commonwealth of Independent States flag, **12**:12

flag of, **9**:8–**9**:9

Ukrainians, **7**:22

Ulster (Ireland), **9**:16

Umm al Qaywayn (United Arab Emirates), **9**:10–**9**:11

UN. *See* United Nations

Union Flag. *See* British Union Flag; Union Jack

Union Islands, **6**:48

Union Jack

Cross of St. George on England's flag, **9**:14

flown by British Virgin Islands, **9**:28, **9**:29

Hong Kong's flag with, **3**:18

Isle of Man and, **9**:40

national flag of England, **9**:14–**9**:15

national flag of Northern Ireland, **9**:16–**9**:17

national flag of Scotland, **9**:18–**9**:19

national flag of Wales, **9**:20–**9**:21

on Anguilla's flag, **9**:22, **9**:23

on Bermuda's flag, **9**:24, **9**:25

on British Blue Ensign, **9**:52–**9**:53

on British Columbia's flag, **2**:38, **2**:39

on British Indian Ocean Territory's flag, **9**:26, **9**:27

on British Red Ensign, **9**:54–**9**:55

on Cayman Islands' flag, **9**:30, **9**:31

on Falkland Islands' flag, **9**:32, **9**:33

on Fiji's flag, **4**:14, **4**:15

on Hawaii's flag, **10**:30, **10**:31

on Montserrat's flag, **9**:42–**9**:43

on Pitcairn Islands Group flag, **9**:44, **9**:45

on Saint Helena's flag, **9**:46, **9**:47

on South Georgia and South Sandwich Island's flag, **9**:48, **9**:49

on Turks and Caicos Islands' flag, **9**:50, **9**:51

on Tuvalu's flag, **8**:60, **8**:61

of United Kingdom, **9**:12–**9**:13

on U.S. flag, **10**:8

Union mark or symbol, **6**:56, **8**:34

Union of Soviet Socialist Republics (USSR). *See also* Soviet Union

flag of, **7**:38–**7**:39, **12**:56, **12**:57

Russia in, **7**:34

UNIP (United National Independence Party), **11**:68

United Arab Emirates (UAE), flag of, **9**:10–**9**:11

United Arab Republic (UAR) flag of, **3**:58

Syria in, **8**:38

United Kingdom

Alberta and, **2**:36

Anguilla, **9**:22–**9**:23

Antigua and Barbuda and, **1**:18

Australia and, **1**:24

Bahamas and, **1**:50

Barbados and, **1**:56

Belize and, **2**:8

Bermuda, **9**:24–**9**:25

Botswana as protectorate, **2**:18

British Blue Ensign, **9**:52–**9**:53

British Columbia's flag and, **2**:38

British Indian Ocean Territory, **9**:26–**9**:27

British Red Ensign, **9**:54–**9**:55

British Virgin Islands, **9**:28–**9**:29

Canada and, **2**:34

Cayman Islands, **9**:30–**9**:31

Christmas Island and, **1**:42

Commonwealth of Nations flag, **12**:13

Cook Islands and, **6**:44

Cyprus and, **3**:38

Dominica and, **3**:50

Egypt as British protectorate, **3**:58

England, **9**:14–**9**:15

Falkland Islands, **9**:32–**9**:33

Faroe Islands and, **3**:44

Fiji and, **4**:14

flag of, **9**:12–**9**:13

Gambia and, **4**:24

Ghana and, **4**:30

Gibraltar, **9**:34–**9**:35

Grenada and, **4**:34

Guernsey, **9**:36–**9**:37

Guyana and, **4**:42

heraldry, **12**:42

Hong Kong, control of, **3**:18

India and, **4**:52

Iraq and, **4**:58

Ireland and, **4**:60

Jersey, **9**:38–**9**:39

Jordan and, **5**:16

Kenya and, **5**:20

Kiribati and, **5**:22

Kuwait and, **5**:28

Lesotho and, **5**:38

Libya and, **5**:42

Malawi as British protectorate, **5**:54

Malaysia and, **5**:56

Malta and, **5**:62

Man, Isle of, **9**:40–**9**:41

Mauritius and, **6**:12

Montana and, **10**:60

Montserrat, **9**:42–**9**:43

Myanmar and, **6**:28

Nepal and, **6**:34

Newfoundland and Labrador and, **2**:44

New South Wales and, **1**:28

British Columbia's flag and, **2**:38

British Indian Ocean Territory, **9**:26–**9**:27

British Red Ensign, **9**:54–**9**:55

British Virgin Islands, **9**:28–**9**:29

New Zealand and, **6**:42

Nigeria and, **6**:54

Niue and, **6**:46

Northern Ireland, **9**:16–**9**:17

Ontario's flag and, **2**:52

Pakistan and, **7**:8

Palestine and, **12**:30

Pitcairn Islands Group, **9**:44–**9**:45

Qatar as British protectorate, **7**:30

Queensland and, **1**:32

Saint Helena, **9**:46–**9**:47

Saint Kitts and Nevis and, **7**:42

Saint Lucia and, **7**:44

Saint Vincent and the Grenadines and, **7**:46

Scotland, **9**:18–**9**:19

Sierra Leone and, **8**:10

Singapore and, **8**:12

Solomon Islands and, **8**:18

Somalia and, **8**:20

Somaliland and, **12**:31

South Australia and, **1**:34

South Georgia and South Sandwich Islands, **9**:48–**9**:49

Sri Lanka and, **8**:26

Sudan and, **8**:28

Suriname and, **8**:30

Swaziland and, **8**:32

Tanzania and, **8**:44

Tasmania and, **1**:36

Tokelau and, **6**:48

Trinidad and Tobago and, **8**:52

Turks and Caicos Islands, **9**:50–**9**:51

Tuvalu and, **8**:60

Uganda and, **8**:62

United Arab Emirates and, **9**:10

Victoria and, **1**:38

Wales, **9**:20–**9**:21

Western Australia and, **1**:40

Zambia and, **11**:68

Zimbabwe and, **11**:70

United National Independence Party (UNIP), **11**:68

United Nations (UN)

East Timor and, **3**:54

Eritrea's flag and, **4**:8

flag of, **12**:24–**12**:25

Somalia and, **8**:20
Taiwan and, **8**:40
United Nations (UN) trust ter-
    ritory, **8**:44
United Nations (UN) Trust
    Territory of the Pacific
    Islands (TTPI)
    Federated States of
        Micronesia, **6**:16
    Marshall Islands, **6**:8
    Northern Mariana Islands,
        11:12
    Palau, **7**:10
United Provinces of Central
    America
    Costa Rica in, **3**:30
    El Salvador's flag and, **3**:60
    Honduras in, **4**:46
    Nicaragua in, **6**:50
United States. *See also* Stars and
    Stripes Flag
    Alabama, **10**:10–**10**:11
    Alaska, **10**:12–**10**:13
    Arizona, **10**:14–**10**:15
    Arkansas, **10**:16–**10**:17
    Azoreans in, **7**:26
    California, **10**:18–**10**:19
    Colorado, **10**:20–**10**:21
    Connecticut, **10**:22–**10**:23
    control of Marshall Islands,
        6:8
    control of Palau, **7**:10
    control of Philippines, **7**:20
    Cuba and, **3**:36
    Delaware, **10**:24–**10**:25
    flag of, **10**:8–**10**:9
    Florida, **10**:26–**10**:27
    Georgia, **10**:28–**10**:29
    Hawaii, **10**:30–**10**:31
    Idaho, **10**:32–**10**:33
    Illinois, **10**:34–**10**:35
    Indiana, **10**:36–**10**:37
    Iowa, **10**:38–**10**:39
    Japan and, **5**:14
    Kansas, **10**:40–**10**:41
    Kentucky, **10**:42–**10**:43
    Liberia and, **5**:40
    Louisiana, **10**:44–**10**:45
    Maine, **10**:46–**10**:47
    Maryland, **10**:48–**10**:49
    Massachusetts, **10**:50–**10**:51
    Michigan, **10**:52–**10**:53
    Minnesota, **10**:54–**10**:55
    Mississippi, **10**:56–**10**:57

Missouri, **10**:58–**10**:59
Montana, **10**:60–**10**:61
Nebraska, **10**:62–**10**:63
Nevada, **10**:64–**10**:65
New Hampshire,
    10:66–**10**:67
New Jersey, **10**:68–**10**:69
New Mexico, **10**:70–**10**:71
New York, **10**:72–**10**:73
North Carolina, **10**:74–**10**:75
North Dakota, **10**:76–**10**:77
Ohio, **10**:78–**10**:79
Oklahoma, **10**:80–**10**:81
Oregon, **10**:82–**10**:83
Panama Canal, **7**:12
Pennsylvania, **10**:84–**10**:85
Rhode Island, **10**:86–**10**:87
South Carolina, **10**:88–**10**:89
South Dakota, **10**:90–**10**:91
South Korea and, **5**:26
Tennessee, **10**:92–**10**:93
Texas, **10**:94–**10**:95
Utah, **10**:96–**10**:97
Vermont, **10**:98–**10**:99
Vietnam War and, **1**:16
Virginia, **10**:100–**10**:101
Washington, **10**:102–**10**:103
Washington, D.C.,
    10:104–**10**:105
West Virginia, **10**:106–**10**:107
Wisconsin, **10**:108–**10**:109
Wyoming, **10**:110–**10**:111
United States, colonial and
    Revolutionary War flags
    Andros Flag, **11**:25
    Bedford Flag, **11**:24
    Eutaw Flag, **11**:34
    Fort Moultrie flag, **11**:33
    Green Mountain Boys flag,
        11:28
    Hopkins flag, **11**:32
    Light Horse of the City of
        Philadelphia flag, **11**:29
    New England flag, **11**:26
    Rhode Island regiment flag,
        11:30
    Taunton Flag, **11**:27
    Washington's Cruisers flag,
        11:31
United States, discovery and
    settlement flags
    Dutch, **11**:21
    English, **11**:20
    French, **11**:19

Russian-American
    Company, **11**:23
    Spanish, **11**:18
    Swedish, **11**:22
United States, flags of 1800's
    Alamo flag, **11**:36
    Bennington Flag, **11**:44
    Bonnie Blue Flag, **11**:39
    California Republic, **11**:38
    Confederate Battle Flag,
        11:41
    Confederate Flag, **11**:43
    Oliver Perry flag, **11**:35
    Stainless Banner, **11**:42
    Stars and Bars, **11**:40
    Texas Navy flag, **11**:37
United States territories
    American Samoa, **7**:48,
        11:8–**11**:9
    Guam, **11**:10–**11**:11
    Northern Mariana Islands,
        11:12–**11**:13
    Puerto Rico, **11**:14–**11**:15
    Virgin Islands of the United
        States, **11**:16–**11**:17
Universal Negro Improvement
    Association, **12**:35
UNO (National Opposition
    Union), **6**:50
UPC (Uganda People's
    Congress), **8**:62
Upolu Island (Samoa), **7**:48
Upper Peninsula (Michigan),
    10:52
Upper Volta, **2**:26
Urdu language, **7**:8
Uruguay, flag of, **11**:54–**11**:55
U.S. Army Institute of Heraldry,
    11:8
U.S. Constitution, **10**:24, **10**:25
U.S. Navy numeral flags, **12**:41
U.S.S. *Arkansas*, **10**:16
USSR. *See* Union of Soviet
    Socialist Republics
Utah, flag of, **10**:96–**10**:97
Uzbekistan, flag of,
    11:56–**11**:57, **12**:12

V

Valdemar II, King of Denmark,
    3:42
Van der Wal, Julien, **7**:46
Vancouver, George, **10**:30
Vanua Levu (Fiji), **4**:14

Vanuatu, flag of, **11**:58–**11**:59
Vatican City, **5**:10; flag of,
    11:60–**11**:61
Vélez Alvarado, Antonio, **11**:14
Velvet Revolution, **8**:14
Venezuela
    flag of, **11**:62–**11**:63
    flag of Ecuador and, **3**:56
Vereenigde Oost-Indische
    Compagnie (United East
    India Company), **11**:21
Verghina (Greece), **5**:50
Vermont
    Bennington Flag, **11**:44
    flag of, **10**:98–**10**:99
    Green Mountain Boys flag,
        11:28
    U.S. flag and, **10**:8
Vexilloid, **9**:20
Victor Emmanuel II, King of
    Italy, **5**:10
Victoria, flag of, **1**:38–**1**:39
Victoria, Queen of England
    authorization of Ontario's
        coat of arms, **2**:52
    coat of arms for Canadian
        provinces, **2**:42
    coat of arms for Nova Scotia,
        2:48
    Queensland flag and, **1**:32
    Victoria and, **1**:38
Vicuña, **7**:18
Vienna (Austria), **1**:46
Viet Cong, **1**:16, **2**:26, **11**:64
Vietnam, flag of, **11**:64–**11**:65
Vietnam War, **1**:16, **2**:26,
    11:64
Vietnamese, **11**:64
Vijaya, Prince of Ceylon, **8**:26,
    12:52
Vikings
    Faroe islanders descendants
        of, **3**:44
    in Massachusetts, **10**:50
    Norwegian, **6**:56
    Swedish, **8**:34
Virgin Gorda (British Virgin
    Islands), **9**:28
Virginia
    flag of, **10**:100–**10**:101
    West Virginia and, **10**:106
Virgin Islands of the United
    States, **9**:28; flag of,
    11:16–**11**:17

Vironia (Estonian students' association), **4**:10
Visayan Islands (Philippines), **7**:20
Viti Levu (Fiji), **4**:14
Vlamingh, Willem de, **1**:40
Volcano, **9**:42

W
Wahhabis, **7**:30, **7**:54
Walachia, **7**:32
Wales
  flag of, **9**:20–**9**:21
  United Kingdom's flag, **9**:12–**9**:13
Walloons, **1**:60
War Council of Iowa, **10**:38
War flag of Bahamas, **1**:50
War of 1812
  Maryland and, **10**:48
  Oliver Perry flag, **11**:35
  Third Maryland Regiment flag, **11**:47
Warrau Indians, **4**:42
Washington (American cruiser), **11**:31
Washington, D.C.
  flag of, **10**:104–**10**:105
  Maryland, **10**:48
Washington, flag of, **10**:102–**10**:103
Washington, George
  colors assigned by, **10**:68
  Continental Colors flag and, **11**:45
  Delaware's flag and, **10**:24
  Washington, D.C. and, **10**:104
  on Washington's flag, **10**:102
Washington, William, **11**:34
Washington's Cruisers flag, **11**:31

Watt, Robert, **2**:50
Weld, Frederick A., **1**:40
Welsh Gaelic, **9**:20
West Bengal, **1**:54
West Caicos Island (Turks and Caicos Islands), **9**:50
West Falkland Island, **9**:32
West Florida Republic, **10**:56
West Germany (German Democratic Republic), **4**:28
West Indies
  Aruba, **6**:38–**6**:39
  Cuba, **3**:36–**3**:37
  Dominican Republic, **3**:52–**3**:53
  Grenada, **4**:34–**4**:35
  Haiti, **4**:44–**4**:45
  Jamaica, **5**:12–**5**:13
  Montserrat, **9**:42–**9**:43
  Netherlands Antilles, **6**:40–**6**:41
  Saint Kitts and Nevis, **7**:42–**7**:43
  Saint Vincent and the Grenadines, **7**:46–**7**:47
  Trinidad and Tobago, **8**:52–**8**:53
  Turks and Caicos Islands, **9**:50–**9**:51
West Virginia, flag of, **10**:106–**10**:107
Western Australia, flag of, **1**:40–**1**:41
Western Sahara flag, **12**:33
White Flag League, **8**:28
Whitehorse (Yukon), **2**:60
White Mountains, **10**:46
Wiles, Isaac, **10**:62
Wilhelmina, Queen of the Netherlands, **6**:36

Willamette Valley (Oregon), **10**:82
William I, Prince of Orange, **6**:36
William I, the Conqueror, **9**:20, **9**:36
Williams, Roger, **10**:86
Wisconsin, flag of, **10**:108–**10**:109
Wolof (ethnic group), **4**:24
Woodland Indians, **10**:38
World Association of Girl Guides and Girl Scouts flag, **12**:27
World Organization of the Scout Movement flag, **12**:26
World War I
  Germany and, **4**:28
  Iowa and, **10**:38
  Poland and, **7**:22
  Samoa and, **7**:48
  Syria during, **8**:38
  Thailand in, **8**:46
  United States and, **10**:8
World War II
  Czech Republic and, **3**:40
  Germany and, **4**:28
  Guam and, **11**:10
  Guernsey occupation during, **9**:36
  Hawaii in, **10**:30
  Indonesia's flag and, **4**:54
  Japan in, **5**:14
  Jersey's occupation during, **9**:38
  Malta and, **5**:62
  Philippines in, **7**:20
  Poland and, **7**:22
  Togo and, **8**:48

United Nations and, **12**:24
United States and, **10**:8
Yugoslavia occupation during, **7**:58
World Zionist Organization congress, **5**:8
Wyoming, flag of, **10**:110–**10**:111
Wythe, George, **10**:100

X
Xiao Hong, **3**:20

Y
Yaksa people, **8**:26
Yangtze river, **3**:16
Yellowstone National Park (Wyoming), **10**:110
Yemen, flag of, **11**:66–**11**:67
Yemen Arab Republic, **11**:66
Yi Song-gye, **5**:26
York, Duke of, **10**:72
Yorktown (Virginia), **10**:100
Yoruba ethnic group, **6**:54
Yugoslavia
  Bosnia-Herzegovina, **2**:16
  Croatia, **3**:34
  Macedonia and, **5**:50
  Serbia and Montenegro, **7**:58
  Slovenia, **8**:16
Yukon, flag of, **2**:60–**2**:61

Z
Zaire. *See* Congo (Kinshasa)
Zambezi River, **11**:68
Zambia, flag of, **11**:68–**11**:69
Zanzibar Island (Tanzania), **8**:44
Zeeland, **6**:36
Zia sun symbol, **10**:70–**10**:71
Zimbabwe, flag of, **11**:70–**11**:71
Zionist flag, **5**:8

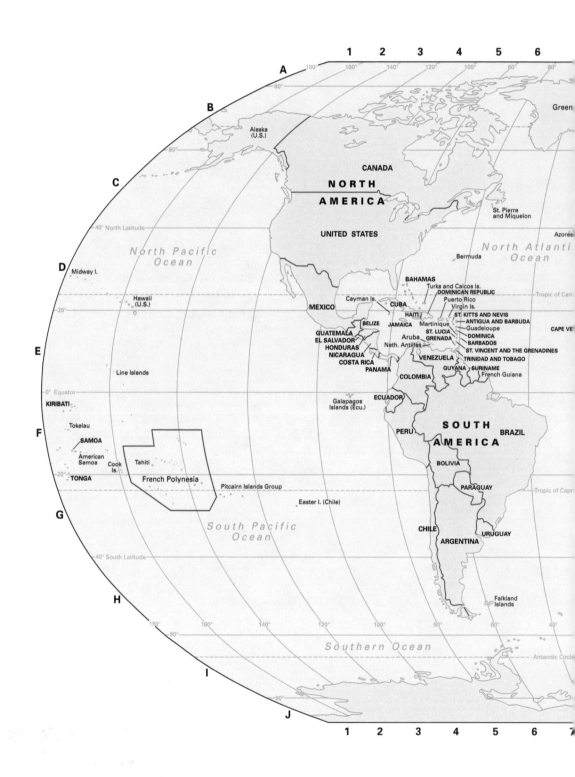

	1	2	3	4	5	6

A

180°   160°   140°   120°   100°   80°   60°

80°

B   Green

Alaska
(U.S.)

60°

CANADA

C

NORTH

AMERICA

St. Pierre
and Miquelon

40° North Latitude

UNITED STATES

Azores

D   Midway I.

*North Pacific
Ocean*

Bermuda

*North Atlanti
Ocean*

Tropic of Can

Hawaii
(U.S.)

20°

BAHAMAS
Turks and Caicos Is.
DOMINICAN REPUBLIC

Cayman Is.   Puerto Rico
CUBA   Virgin Is.

MEXICO

HAITI   ST. KITTS AND NEVIS
ANTIGUA AND BARBUDA
BELIZE   Guadeloupe   **CAPE VE**
JAMAICA   Martinique   ST. LUCIA
DOMINICA

GUATEMALA   Aruba   GRENADA   BARBADOS
EL SALVADOR   ST. VINCENT AND THE GRENADINES
HONDURAS   Neth. Antilles   TRINIDAD AND TOBAGO
NICARAGUA   **VENEZUELA**
COSTA RICA   GUYANA   SURIName
PANAMA   French Guiana
COLOMBIA

E

Line Islands

ECUADOR

0° Equator

Galapagos
Islands (Ecu.)

KIRIBATI

Tokelau

SOUTH

PERU   **AMERICA**   **BRAZIL**

F

SAMOA

American
Samoa   Tahiti   Cook   BOLIVIA
Is.

TONGA   French Polynesia   20°   PARAGUAY   Tropic of Capr

Pitcairn Islands Group

Easter I. (Chile)

G

CHILE   URUGUAY

*South Pacific
Ocean*

ARGENTINA

40° South Latitude

H

180°   160°   140°   120°   100°   80°   60°   40°

Falkland
Islands

I

80°

Southern Ocean

Antarctic Circle

J

80°

1	2	3	4	5	6	7